MARRIAGE: THEOLOGY AND REALITY

Cathy Molloy

Marriage:
Theology
and Reality

First published in 1996 by

the columba press
55A Spruce Avenue,
Stillorgan Industrial Park,
Blackrock, Co Dublin, Ireland

NOVALIS
49 Front Street East, 2nd Floor,
Toronto, Ontario,
Canada M5E 1B3

ISBN 1-85607-166-9

ISBN 2-89088-854-1

Cover by Bill Bolger
Origination by The Columba Press
Printed in Ireland by Genprint Ltd., Dublin

Acknowledgements

I would like to thank everyone who made this book possible. Firstly my family: thanks to Shane for his constant support and encouragement, and to Nessa, Donough, James and Gina for their patience and interest in the project.

The book has its origins in a dissertation submitted in partial fulfillment of the requirements for Licentiate in Theology. I owe a great deal to Gerry O'Hanlon SJ for his unfailing patience, help and encouragement throughout.

I would like to thank especially friends, and my teachers, and the staff at The Milltown Institute of Theology and Philosophy, in particular Edel and Jim, who gave me important advice and much appreciated encouragement at various stages.

Contents

Introduction

Have theologians ever really understood enough of the reality of marriage as they have presented and taught the Christian ideal of marriage from earliest times? Church-speak about marriage can often have an alien ring about it when considered in the light of the daily life of average married couples. Is hearing that your marriage is a sign or symbol of God's love, of the unity of Christ and the church, just about tolerable within the confines of the church building but definitely something we leave behind there as we get on with the business of living, the ups and downs of the shared existence that marriage is? Surely the joys and difficulties, the happy times and the traumas, are the same for everyone, and religion or faith, or the absence of it, has very little if anything to do with the real issues? Setting out to look at contemporary marriage in relation to traditional theology and, more particularly to recent theology of marriage, the question at once arises as to whether the two are in touch with one another at all, and, if they are, to what extent?

For many reasons, modern marriage is perceived to be an institution in crisis. Daily in the media we see, hear and read treatments of the key issues. The breakdown statistics continue to rise at unprecedented rates, and the effects on individuals, (children in particular), families, and society in general are constantly debated in terms of the wellbeing or suffering of those directly involved and, more recently, in terms of the financial cost to the state. The fundamental issue of commitment presents real problems in our culture, and not just in relation to marriage. Questions such as marital fidelity, the decision to have children or not (or indeed the incapacity to have children due to infertility which is widespread and by all accounts growing), fair play between partners and the issue of conflict and how and whether it is resolved, are the substance of the daily living of married couples. Their connection with the categories of theology can seem tenuous indeed.

A criticism of theology of marriage as we have known it might be that it deals almost exclusively with the two ends of the spectrum. The ideal – of faithful, permanent, and peaceful committed existence of husband, wife and children – to be aimed at, is often presented as though it were the readily available reality for most people, as though *wanting* to achieve this unity which is the image of Christ and the church is all that is needed to make it *actual*. At the opposite end, marriage breakdown has always been addressed in terms of the dramatic – divorce is never to be permitted, the covenant sign may not be broken whatever about the inward reality that it is supposed to signify. Whether in terms of sacrament, of law and institution, or, more recently, of compassion and appropriate care for those involved in breakdown, marriage theology has focused almost exclusively on the heroic and the disastrous. Ordinary Catholics with their ordinary marriages might justifiably wonder where they fit into the picture.

What does our church teaching offer to the average couple as they set out with the same or perhaps even higher expectations, in terms of their mutual love and hopes for personal fulfillment, as those embarking on marriage have always done? What does it say to those same couples about their understandable fears and anxieties concerning a commitment into the future to a way of life that can seem threatened, if not under siege, by many aspects of the changing world in which we live? Do recent cultural changes contribute greatly to the distance which may be perceived between theological language and some of its concepts and the marriages of average Catholics?

The starting point for this study is marriage as traditionally and presently understood, and marriage as understood in Christian theology. The second chapter examines the basis of this theology in scripture and the tradition, with particular emphasis on the Old Testament *Song of Songs* and how its interpretation may have been significant for the way theology developed. In the third chapter, recent theology of marriage is considered with a somewhat detailed look at the developments to be observed in particular contemporary theologians. The final chapter attempts to draw together the theology and the lived reality of marriage, and to note what may or may not be helpful for people today in the light of the issues mentioned above. In doing this, the sociological aspects of marriage have been interpreted within a theological perspective. Praxis, reflection on the experience of marriage, has been an important element in the overall presentation of this work, and I hope that the judgements it contains are not much the less objective on that account.

Fundamental to the topic is interpersonal love and what it means in marriage, as one way of loving in the world. Within a faith perspective, all human loving has its source in God and reflects something of the love of God for humanity. In a discussion about marriage, it is appropriate to acknowledge the other ways of loving that express human giving; the many loving relationships of men and women that are not marriage; the dedicated, specific kind of love that chosen celibacy can bring to our world; the love of single people that often goes unnamed. All contribute to the building up of love in the world and all are to be valued.

In Christian marriage the theology and the living cannot be separated. The shortfall between the ideals presented and the reality of individual marriages is ever present. Questions arise about models, absolutes, hopes and dreams, in the face of the existential reality. The experience of wanting to risk all with and for the partner, and at the same time, the awareness of the unreality of this because of many other factors in contemporary life, adds to the difficulty of living the Christian ideal of mutual love without limit. For Christians, the unlimited love of Christ is there as example. Ideally we too can love in an unlimited way. But what is the reality? Can ordinary men and women love like this habitually? Often? Sometimes? Rarely? Perhaps the most the average married couple can hope for is *sometimes* to be this way. The group of two is part of a wider group. And the wider group, family, society, the wider world, impinges far more than we are conscious of.

The question of the symbols which relate to marriage and who decides on their appropriateness, given that they are such powerful carriers of meaning, may contribute to contemporary problems. Perhaps there is need to look for new ones. It has been suggested that the challenge be offered in categories of people's own experience and not in an ideology alien to it.[1] Is the love of Christ for the church an alien category for those about to be married today? Does its suitability depend too much on a degree of faith on the part of individuals that is simply not there for many, or too difficult to sustain in today's world?

What of the attempt at unity that marriage involves? Does this attempt by each to get into the mind of the other, the body of the other, the spirit of the other, and the radical impossibility of this that must be faced before a realistic kind of unity can be achieved, leave room for questions about the oneness we seek? Does the fact that we seem always to strive for more, for what is not possible in our humanness, imply something about human desire generally, in its source and in its goal? What of the question of dependency, physical and psychological, and the need to go beyond this to love freely? These then are some of the underlying questions raised, in the hope of clarifying somewhat their place in our marriages and in our theology in a way that might be enriching to both.

CHAPTER 1

Marriage and Christian Marriage

THE TRADITIONAL MEANING OF MARRIAGE

The precise content and meaning of the life shared by men and women that is marriage cannot be defined. Research into its history in different cultures reveals no clear picture of the reality.[1] Was polygamy the earliest form of marriage? Did the modern understanding of marriage as monogamous evolve, or was monogamy the original? Is there something unchanging about the nature of marriage, or does the fact that it has expressed itself in a variety of forms throughout the stages of human history indicate that there are no absolutes with regard to its content and meaning?

It is often pointed out that sexuality has always been characterised by a vagueness and openness that is given form and definition by society.[2] Western culture, and so also marriage, has been deeply influenced by the teaching of the Christian tradition which aimed to integrate marriage into its understanding of humanity and the world. In this view, human sexuality was incorporated into personal love and self-giving by the mutual love and faithfulness of the two spouses. Marriage was a form of partnership which involved what Augustine, in the fifth century, had identified as three goods: children, fidelity and permanence. It was the appropriate form of the expression of human sexuality in the overall view of humanity and the world.[3]

Through the progressive alignment of church and state in the West, marriage evolved as a personal/religious and social reality at once, the experience of a particular kind of shared existence with particular elements, goals, expectations. At the same time it was a social institution that had a legal definition with specific rights and duties, which came to be regulated by the state through civil law and by many religious traditions by means of particular rites and ceremonies.[4]

In practice, traditionally marriage was a community within the extended family. Prior to the industrial revolution, the world of marriage and family and that of work would not have had clear boundaries. The public and private spheres of life were not well delineated and social relationships took precedence over personal life. Although love was not precluded, people married for more objective considerations and a clear distinction existed between love before or outside of marriage and marital love itself. The more important factor was that marriage gave the partners a clearly defined place in the objective social order. This dictated the function and role of the couple from the outside, while the personal and subjective was present as background but, in the order of things, was secondary.[5]

If the line between the world of work and that of family was not well drawn, what was clear was the function and role of the partners in a marriage. The outward aspects of life and work were the concern of the husband, while the wife bore the children and was responsible for their upbringing and the domestic side of life. Whether marriages were based on love or arranged for other purposes, the basic pattern remained the same. Marriage involved commitment and a particular way of life to ensure the wellbeing of the spouses and children, and exclusivity and permanence of relationship were accepted as necessary requirements.[6]

CONTEMPORARY MARRIAGE

With the advent of industrialisation and the move to a more urbanised society, the ties linking marriage and the family to the world of work and community have been severed. Gradually many of the functions performed by the family and extended family have been taken over by the state. The married couple, instead of becoming automatically part of an existing stable community which would give a firm foundation and stability to married life, find themselves alone and virtually isolated amongst the various sectors of society.[7]

What is the lived reality that is marriage in our day? As the way of life of the majority, marriage, while retaining its central meaning as the committed, lifelong sharing of existence of a man and woman, has changed dramatically as a result of the developments in human living referred to above, and perhaps to an unanticipated degree due to the more recent advances in technology this century. The struggle for material survival has diminished significantly for very many people (in the West at least); basic health care and housing have become the concern of the state, and even the recent phenomenon of large scale unemployment does not leave people materially destitute as it would have at other stages. With increased availability of reliable contraceptive methods, the number of children per family has decreased and their education is largely taken care of outside the home.

Perhaps the most significant factor of all is the evolution, or even revolution, in the position of women. The status of women in society has changed, with at least a theoretical equality of educational and employment opportunity, which has led to a much altered view of their possible contribution. This in turn has brought about new dimensions to the husband/wife relationship and new ways of parenting. While still being mainly the concern of mothers, the care of infants and young children increasingly involves fathers.

With regard to the world of the couple, the material aspects of life being generally satisfied at a basic level, there is new emphasis on the quality of personal life and the inter-personal life of the married couple in particular. This may be seen as a reversal of the traditional situation, but also as the occasion of greater freedom in the personal and subjective aspect of married life.[8]

The stability and security, which formerly existed as a matter of course, now has to be achieved by the couple themselves. The loss of function, and change in structure, of family presents a challenge which may be seen as threatening to marriage on the one hand, but which also is the means of marriage based on an interpersonal relationship, on mutual love and a fundamental equality of the partners. Modern marriage could be said to be democratic. Negatively, however, the fact that modern marriage and the family are more removed from the extended family of former times, with its strong neighbourhood networks, means the couple is deprived of sources of support and companionship outside the marriage and experiences a heavy burden to be all things to each other. With the emphasis on the inner person, which is so characteristic of our culture, and its consequent expectation of a high degree of personal fulfilment, it is clear that marriage has become a potentially more rewarding, but also potentially more unstable, state than heretofore.

A factor which is very important to the analysis is the extent to which people are living longer than before. Couples may expect to have many years of life together after their family has left home.[9] Developments in psychology illuminate aspects of life in terms of phases, and the life of a married couple into old age is a feature of modern writing on marriage.

The sexual liberation which is characteristic of our time is another important influence on contemporary marriage. Sexual fulfilment is rightly sought by both partners at the heart of marriage, and there is a refreshing openness about this in relation to women as well as men. However, this basic human desire is often exploited in our society to the extent that sexual expression becomes at times a commodity that everyone should have, or something that may be used to get something else. Marriage no less than other human relationships is affected by this atmosphere in our culture. On the one hand, there is the new openness and acceptance of the joy and fulfilment to be experienced in sexual relationship and, on the other, there is the de-personalisation of sex, the separation of sex from love, the instrumentalisation of sex. In its positive aspect, people may be helped or encouraged to greater fulfilment as loving sexual persons, but there is also the negative side which tends to exploitation and may contribute to the higher incidence of child sexual abuse and rape or violent sexual assault which is emerging.[10]

Perhaps the most notable difference between contemporary and traditional marriage concerns the question of children. The average family now has two or less children. Efficient contraception means that the timing of the births can be chosen, and some couples choose not to have children at all and to put their energies entirely into their careers. There is a view that sees contraception as a mixed blessing, since 'with the fear of pregnancy removed, there is little to oppose pre- and extra-marital sex.'[11]

THE BREAKDOWN OF MARRIAGE

Stability is not a strong feature of contemporary marriage. What are the factors perceived to work directly or indirectly against stable marriage? With the introduction of relatively liberal divorce laws in most Western societies over the past thirty years, the number of marriages ending in divorce has increased markedly. One study written in 1986 suggested that, if the present trends continued, up to forty per cent of marriages in England and Wales would end in divorce by the end of the century.[12] Whether the change is due to marriage being under greater stress as a result of the cultural factors referred to, or because unsatisfactory marriages are less likely to be endured, or whether it is due to the availability of divorce, cannot be ascertained. Changed roles within marriage, changed work and career patterns, certainly play a part in the outcome – for example, the reality of a clash between family ideals and work roles is a significant source of conflict in middle class life.[13]

There is also a feminist view of marriage which sees it as inherently oppressive for women. This, for many, has led to a perceived need at least to change, if not to break down, the institution of the family as it has been understood, and has lessened the commitment of many women to their marriage.

The above brief survey represents something of the reality of the context in which marriage is lived today. Christian marriage belongs right in the middle of this, and the question arises as to whether it is any different from marriage as already described.

CHRISTIAN MARRIAGE

Is marriage between Christians different from that which is described in the previous paragraphs? Does the fact that marriage for Christians is a sacrament mean that, because of Christ, the meaning of marriage is altered? Christian marriage is not a special sort of pairing, but rather ordinary human marriage which takes on new meaning because of the faith and baptism of the spouses. Marriage in the Christian church is built on the secular reality that is marriage in whatever culture, and yet is not entirely determined by that secular culture. All marriage is first the sign of the love and unity of the couple. For Christians it has the added meaning of being part of the creation/saving plan of God, of being a sign of the covenant love of God for humanity. The church teaches that, for those who are baptised, marriage is further distinct in that it symbolises the love and unity of Christ and the church. Because of the faith and baptism of the spouses their marriage is drawn into the reality of that love and unity. Nonethless, the human reality that marriage is, is also Christian marriage, so its treatment in theology will evolve as the reality evolves.

The qualities of Christian marriage are based on the Old and New Testament command, 'You shall love your neighbour as yourself'.[14] This love is defined in the Old Testament in terms of loyalty, service, and obedience rather than interpersonal affection. The Letter to the Ephesians (chap 5) describes it as a mutual giving way, and in the Letter to the Corinthians love does not insist on its own way, the goal being that the two persons become one body as in the first book of the Old Testament, Genesis 2:18-25. Love is also mutual service in a Christian marriage since, as Christians, both spouses are to be imitators of Christ who came not to be served but to serve (Mk 10:4-5).

In Christian marriage, love is faithful, the spouses are to love one another as Christ loved the church, as in the Old Testament Hosea loved Gomer (Hos 2:14-21). This mutually faithful love indicates that Christian marriage be permanent and exclusive. The indissolubility that emerges is a quality of Christian love. The living out of this kind of love is the challenge and task of the Christian husband and wife.

So Christian marriage is distinct in that its source and goal is the particular love that Christ showed: the faithful, serving, enduring love with which he is united to the church. Does it look like an impossible ideal for today's Christian spouses, given the cultural realities on which all marriage is based? Is talk of love of Christ for the church, of exclusivity and permanence modelled on such a covenant partnership, helpful or even meaningful for today's Christians who struggle, like all other married people, with the kinds of relationships that are contemporary marriage? Christian spouses, just as any others, have to live with the fact of breakdown of the marriage relationship, whether this ends in separation or annulment or divorce. The legal and religious difficulties surrounding second or subsequent relationships, with the decisions about whether or when to have children and the means to achieve this, are also the problems of Christians today, as is the conflict between the Christian view of sexuality and that prevailing in our culture.

CHRISTIAN MARRIAGE AS SACRAMENT

What does the Roman Catholic Church mean when it claims marriage is a sacrament? What might the sacramentality of marriage mean to Christian spouses living their particular marriages? Many people will be familiar with the description of sacrament as 'an outward sign of an inward reality'. Sacrament may also be described as 'a prophetic symbol with which the church, the Body of Christ, proclaims and makes real and celebrates for believers that presence and action of God which is called *grace*'. The Roman Catholic Church holds that marriage is such a prophetic symbol.[15] What does this mean for marriage? The issue of precisely how, in the life of the couple, this may be brought about and sustained, through what actions, will be developed in a later section. The basic point is that marriage of Christians is for them a means of proclaiming, making real and celebrating the presence and action of God. Human persons loving one another humanly, but with the kind of love to which Christians aspire, involves a double reality. Christian marriage firstly *symbolises* the love that is between the couple, but it also actualises, through this human love and its different modes of expression, the presence of God to humanity, of Christ to the church. Their marriage is capable of being constitutive of God's saving plan for humanity. However, this possibility is not automatically realised. Karl Rahner, writing about marriage as sacrament, points out that grace must be accepted in freedom.[16]

When the faith required for the free acceptance of grace, as understood by Rahner, is absent, such a marriage can be an invalid or ineffective sacrament. This is a point which is very significant for marriage of the baptised today and for those attempting to deal with the reality of breakdown. The significance arises because of the many baptised but *unbelieving* Christians in our contemporary world and the sacramentality of marriage as traditionally viewed. That fidelity and permanence are part of the sacramental sign of Christian marriage means that exclusivity and indissolubility cannot be compromised and, according to the teaching of the church, the solution to breakdown must be sought elsewhere than in divorce.

In the cases where this faith, as described by Rahner, is present, what does sacramentality say to Christian spouses? It says that 'matter matters';[17] that the physical is 'essentially the vehicle of the spiritual, not an irrelevant or unsatisfactory appendage to it'; that our ordinary marriage, in its attempt at oneness that must be physical and spiritual at once, is 'by the action of God opened to the immediacy of God himself'.[18] Such is the dignity of the personal love between married people. This is the Christian view of love, sexually expressed in marriage, which has not always been explicitly so considered in the tradition of our church. The new life that is part of the giving and receiving of love between human persons, and that has at times in our history been seen as the only justification for the joy that is God-given in sexual fulfilment, is not seen as a separate element in the Christian view of married love. It is however distinct, and contemporary Christian theology of marriage perhaps focuses deliberately on the personal love of the couple rather than on its possible, if almost always hoped for, outcome. Whether this is a necessary redressing of the balance after the almost exclusive emphasis on the procreative in our tradition, or whether it reflects the move to personalist considerations of our culture, is not clear. What is clear to Christian theologians is that, in the present cultural conditions, marriage as in the Christian ideal can only continue to survive if the greatest attention is paid to the relationship of the couple as couple, and its centrality to all other aspects of marriage.

This brings the question of another aspect of sacramentality to the fore. Sacrament is, in the case of marriage, ritual or rite *and* the ongoing life of the couple. But sacraments are also described as prayers of the church, of the community of believers. The community aspect of sacrament is receiving new attention in the life of Christians. The couple must leave father and mother and be joined and become one body, as Genesis understands God to have ordained. But, more than ever today, they will do well to remember that they are also one body in Christ. Every couple is part of the Christian community and the re-establishing of the ecclesial dimension, which is being worked for today, may yet be the most significant factor in the preservation of the institution of marriage in the church.

The attempt in this chapter has been to set Christian marriage in its contemporary cultural context; to indicate that ordinary human marriage is precisely what Christian marriage is, but with another dimension whose basis is faith; to point out, in initial form, the sacramental ideal which is the foundation for what can seem the very ambitious project of such marriage; and to set the background for the question as to whether the theology of marriage does in fact reflect, or even address, the reality as experienced by Christians today. To do this, it is necessary to give a brief account of marriage theology in the tradition which is the root and basis of modern theology of marriage, and this will be the matter of the next chapter.

CHAPTER 2

Theology of Marriage
in the Tradition

THE OLD TESTAMENT

The Jews of the Old Testament were different from their contemporaries in that their faith was in *one* God. Monotheism had implications for every aspect of life. Specifically with regard to marriage, the Old Testament has not so much a theology of marriage, as that this most ordinary of human relationships is revealed in a new way in the light of the whole of life lived in covenant relationship with the Creator God.[1]

Among other peoples in the ancient Near East, worship of fertility gods, gods who controlled the forces of nature and the force of life, was the norm. Sexuality and all it involved was seen as a mysterious gift and fertility was ensured by means of magic rites and temple prostitution. The Old Testament reveals traces of the development from polytheism, through henotheism (belief in a particular god, for example of this or that place), to the monotheism that distinguished the Hebrew people from their neighbours. The Jews placed themselves directly under the care of the one God from whom everything in creation came. This led to an idea of marriage in which sexuality and fertility were removed from the sphere of the cults. Marriage was a human reality and worldly. It was worldly in the sense that the world was God's work and gift to humanity. Creation itself gave marriage its holy dimension.

The two creation accounts in Genesis express belief in the nature of human persons as relational. The older account, Genesis 2:18-25, shows that man and woman together are humanity as God intended. Whether in near or distant relationship, according to Karl Barth, each sex is itself in relation to the other.[2] Although this account of creation has often been used to support the notion of the superiority of the man over the woman, some theologians see in it the equal value of male and female. Sexual difference clearly forms an essential part of humanity's created being.[3] This being so, the radical equality of man and woman must be the basis for any understanding of the relationship, however much mystery is part of it.

The second account, in the first chapter of Genesis, reinforces the equality of the sexes. Male and female are created in the image of God. In this second narrative, the relationship having been established, their recognition of one another as 'one body' is blessed by God with the possibility of new life. This gift of the possibility of children is at once linked to and yet quite distinct from the joining of husband and wife. According to Jack Dominian 'these realities are separate and between them contain the appropriate possibilities of the man-woman relationship in marriage.'[4] In spite of the disorder that comes into the relationship (Gen 3:7) because of their sin, the effects of which are ever present between them, the fundamental goodness of the gift of sex and its possibility for children remains. In spite of the difficulties now inherent in the striving for the original relationship, 'a monogamous relationship orientated towards procreation' is upheld in many books of the Old Testament.[5]

In the whole of scripture, the *Song of Songs* is singular in its treatment of the man/woman relationship in the language and concepts of erotic love. This description of the joy and beauty of love between a man and a woman, the essential goodness of maleness and femaleness as attracting and attracted, as desiring and desired, loving and loved, bearing in mind the overall context of creation as God's gift, reminds us of the ideal that might be achieved. It reminds us too that with this love and its expression as the basis of the marriage relationship, the harmony, peace and contentment of the first couple in Genesis may be aspired to. The fact that the *Song* is without moral overtones, does not include reference to procreation, and was held in the canons of scripture with some opposition, must be seen as testimony to the fundamental Christian belief in the goodness of human sexual love in itself, for all the negative consideration to which it has been subjected intermittently.[6] This will be treated in more detail later.

In the Wisdom books marriage is seen to be good for the man who fears Yahweh. There are many references to the good wife, and a happy marriage is a blessing from God.[7] In Sirach 26:1, 3, 'a good wife is a great blessing; she will be granted among the blessings of the man who fears Yahweh.' The patriarchal nature of the society in which the Wisdom books were written is particularly well illustrated by the references to marriage, where a wife is significant only in so far as she may add to or detract from the blessings of her husband. There are warnings against infidelity and adultery, and the value of many children (regarded by the Jews as a blessing from Yahweh) is seen in relation to the faith of the parents.[8]

A concrete example of the Old Testament ideal of marriage is found in the book of Tobit. The marriage of Tobias and Sarah is begun with Tobit, her father, asking the Lord's favour for the couple. Their married life together begins with prayers of Sarah and Tobias for the grace and protection of God. They value their marriage relationship but it is relativised in the light of their intimate relationship with God and their desire to live according to God's will.[9] In spite of their natural wish to consummate their marriage, they first spend time praying together. So faith and religion for the Jews had a concrete effect on marriage as on every aspect of life. The religious dimension to marriage is gradually uncovered and was most developed by Hosea the prophet and his reference to marriage as symbol of the covenant between Yahweh and his people.

It was almost inevitable that among the Jewish people marriage would be seen as symbolising the covenant love between God and his people.[10] Yahweh is their God and they are his people (Deut 26:17-19); together they form a community of grace, of salvation, of one body. Hosea the prophet was first to speak of the covenant relationship in terms of marriage, and specifically in the example of his own marriage to Gomer, a temple prostitute, and of his fidelity to her in spite of her unfaithfulness. The marriage of Hosea and Gomer is presented as a real marriage, but in it Hosea sees a symbol of the covenant relationship between Yahweh and Israel. Just as Yahweh continues to love the people of Israel in spite of their turning to other gods, Hosea redeems Gomer, buys her back, after she has abandoned him for another (Hos 3:1-5). The covenant, and God's activity within it, became the model for Hosea's own marriage. A permanent rupture was not possible in the light of God's love for Israel, and with a tangible prophetic action Hosea took Gomer back.

A deeper meaning of marriage, of this particular marriage, is revealed here. This is a prophetic form of marriage, not present on its own account but because it is the object of a call from God. Marriage as secular reality and as institution, is a symbol and representation of Yahweh's constant love for his people.[11] The primary and clear meaning here is that Yahweh is faithful. But a second meaning is also present. The meaning of marriage is not only the loving union of a man and a woman, but also 'a prophetic symbol, proclaiming and making real in representative image the steadfast love of Yahweh for Israel.'[12] Jeremiah, Ezekiel and Isaiah also see marriage as symbolising the covenant love of Yahweh for Israel.[13]

There is an important point to be noted here. The meaning does not progress from human marriage to divine covenant, but the other way around. Belief in and experience of covenant love and fidelity creates the belief in, and the possibility of, this kind of love and fidelity in marriage, which then and only then becomes a prophetic symbol of the covenant. This invites the question as to whether ignoring or underestimating this fact has led to much of the difficulty experienced in dealing with marriage and indissolubility. Is it simply meaningless to expect people who have no sense of the prior love of God, and perhaps even no faith in such a possibility, to take on the notion of marriage as indissoluble sacrament, even though they have been baptized? The 'I hate divorce, says Yahweh … so do not be faithless' of Malachi 2:16 is in the context of a prior experience of the steadfast love of Yahweh which gives new meaning to all experience, and in a particular way to marriage. The covenant theme is to be taken up and further developed by Paul in the New Testament notion of Christian marriage as image of the love and unity between Christ and the church.

THE NEW TESTAMENT

To look for instances of marriage being singled out in the synoptic gospel accounts would be to misunderstand the place of marriage in Jewish life at the time of Jesus. It seems that marriage did not concern Jesus greatly. Certainly the miracle at Cana was the first public action of Jesus that led people to wonder who he was, but his words about marriage and divorce in Mark 10:11-12, Matthew 5:32, 19:9, and Luke 16:18 are part of an exchange provoked by others, who were more interested in encouraging him to take sides between two rabbinic schools than in marriage itself.[14] Marriage was a basic reality of life, taken for granted. In Jewish understanding, the first command of God to the first man and woman was 'increase and multiply'. To ensure the continuance of the family, the first duty of people was to marry. Celibacy was considered an anomaly, even a disgrace.[15]

On this account perhaps it is not surprising that, in the synoptic gospels, marriage is discussed only in terms of the divorce question. Divorce was permitted among the Jews and for strictly or liberally interpreted causes. The teaching of Jesus was to challenge radically the acceptance of divorce and to propose marriage as an indissoluble union. In Matthew 19:8 Jesus sees the existence of divorce as a concession by Moses to the hardness of heart of the people. Adultery too is out of the question, and in this regard also Jesus shows himself to be as concerned with the inner attitudes of the heart as with the outward actions (Mt 5:28).[16]

What is this marriage that Jesus teaches is permanent and exclusive? In the letters to the Corinthians and the Ephesians, marriage for followers of Christ, and the kind of love on which it is based, is described. Paul sees marriage in which the love of husband and wife can image that between Christ and the church as part of 'the great mystery' (Eph 5:25-27). Developing the symbolism of Hosea, Paul points out that through relationship with Christ Christian marriage is taken into the creative, redemptive plan of God to unite all people and all things in God. From here Christian theologians would later deduce that Christian marriage is a sacrament and as such absolutely indissoluble. If Christian husbands and wives love one another as Christ loves, then the marriage relationship can be redeemed, and the unity, equality of dignity, harmony, fidelity and so on implied in Genesis can be restored, and the hardness of heart which followed the fall, necessitating divorce, can be overcome.

The writer of Ephesians extends the analogy to the question of order in the relationship – the headship of Christ over the church being seen as model for headship of husbands over wives. Although the context is one of mutual subordination, the question must be asked as to how realistic it is to transpose some of the verses in this passage to our modern culture where anything that suggests hierarchy based on male superiority is anathema to so many women, and hopefully to most men. Elizabeth Schüssler Fiorenza, in referring to the hermeneutical problem with the Pauline subordination text, points out that some feminist writers argue that early Christianity was already sexist and so a revisionist feminist interpretation must fail. Others see in the same Pauline text, correctly understood and interpreted, support for women's equality and dignity, while still others see them as 'situation variable and therefore script but not scripture'...[17] The notion of subordination evokes today many of the worst features of male domination over women which has been tolerated, and many believe even encouraged, by our church over the centuries. Throughout the history of our patriarchal institution this passage has been exploited to justify a view of marriage that needed the subordination of women in order to work. The power of the church has been behind this theology, and only in recent times have men and women begun to free themselves from its hold. The letter of Pope John Paul II, addressed to women in advance of the UN's Fourth World Conference on Women in Beijing, represents an important step in bringing about necessary change.

What else do we learn of Christian marriage from Paul? That the love described in Ephesians 5:21-33, modelled on Christ's love for the church, is primarily a unifying love. The love of Christ, the *bridegroom*, is for the church, the *bride*. Love here is not a means to an end, the beloved is not a means to the existence of someone or something else. The love that unites seeks only the perfection and well-being of the beloved, and in this love married people are acceptable to and loved by God.[18]

In 1 Corinthians 7, Paul's view on the relative goodness of marriage in light of the expected second coming of Christ (the end of the world as known to them) is quite clear. It is better to remain unmarried as he is. He sees marriage as a concession to human weakness. It is better to marry than to burn (1 Cor 7:9). There is difference of opinion among scholars concerning the meaning of this text. Some see Paul as recommending marriage as a lesser evil for those who have not the strength to remain celibate. Others under-

stand Paul to say that if someone cannot accept celibacy
they should see in this fact a call from God; they should
make a vocation of it.[19] Marriage, even in this second interpretation, appears negatively presented. Whether or not
marriage is a vocation, celibacy is the primary value according to Paul. In his opinion only the unmarried can
give their mind entirely to the Lord's affairs and how to
please the Lord. The married person is divided in mind
and, by implication, incapable of being holy in body and
spirit, which is what should be sought by Christians. Yet
Paul is aware of the reality of the desire of men and
women for one another and teaches that to avoid immoral-
ity every man should have his own wife and every woman
her own husband (1 Cor 7:2-5).[20] Those who are married
must not separate, according to the Lord's ruling, but he
himself sees that there is a case for separation when the
unbelieving partner of a believer is unwilling to stay in
peace. In this case, and he is aware that it is his own rule
and not that of Jesus, not only is separation permissable
but the Christian partner is not bound to the marriage.

Paul's views on marriage, taken as a whole, seem confusing and even contradictory. Marriage is clearly a second
best option for the believer and yet it may be that spouses
are the means of salvation for one another (1 Cor 7:16). But
there is no inherent contradiction here. His reasons for
proposing virginity or celibacy as a better way of life are
his own, as he points out in verse 25. In the light of the expected end of the world, it would seem practical and logical advice. It is not that marriage is not good, but that in
particular circumstances celibacy and virginity are better.
Both are gifts and everyone has been given his/her own. It
would seem that the more important point is the relationship of the believer to God. The choice of a way of life, or
continuing in a way of life, is dependent on the personal
conversion of the individual. Here it seems appropriate to
ask whether much of the misunderstanding about the different states in Christian life is as a result of their being
treated independently of particular persons and of the

personal faith of every individual. This is not to suggest that there is a foolproof way of discovering what one's particular vocation is. Karl Barth writes, 'There is a genuine Christian obedience which does not lead a man into marriage but past it.' And:

> 'there is a genuine Christian obedience in the decision to marry only when the Christian objections to marriage are honestly weighed and there is thus a true choice and acceptance of marriage as a matter of special gift and vocation, as a step which may and must be taken in the same freedom and constraint of the Spirit in which it is not taken by others.'[21]

This suggests that both marriage and chosen celibacy, in view of the 'divine command' (as Barth calls the genuine attempt to live according to God's will), are equally calls of God and should be taken equally seriously as far as the individual's stance before God is concerned. One might pose the question here whether marriage would be so readily entered into by so many if the same care was given to marriage as a state in Christian life as is given to the discernment and nurturing of vocation to priesthood or religious life.

At this point I return to the *Song of Songs* and what became of it in our tradition, because it seems to me critical in the Christian attitude to marriage, celibacy and virginity. As already indicated, the *Song of Songs* is a joyful celebration of love between man and woman, with particular emphasis on the delight of this love physically expressed. Mutuality is the order of this relationship with the woman as free as the man in expressing desire and passion for the beauty of the beloved. This beauty of the lovers, their desire for one another and fulfilment in one another, are seen as God's creation gifts. Towards the end of the *Song* the man wonders at the beauty of his beloved:

> How beautiful, how entrancing you are,
> my loved one, daughter of delights!
> You are stately as a palm tree,
> and your breasts are like clusters of fruit.

I said, 'Let me climb up into the palm
to grasp its fronds.'
May I find your breasts like clusters
of grapes on the vine,
your breath sweet-scented like apples,
your mouth like fragrant wine
flowing smoothly to meet my caresses,
gliding over my lips and teeth.[22]

The woman responds:
I am my beloved's, his longing is all for me.
Come, my beloved, let us go out into the fields
to lie among the henna bushes;
let us go early to the vineyards
and see if the vine has budded or its blossom opened,
or if the pomegranates are in flower.
There I shall give you my love,
when the mandrakes yield their perfume,
and all choice fruits are ready at our door,
fruits new and old
which I have in store for you my love.[23]

Biblical scholars are divided as to who was the first
Patristic writer to interpret the song as allegory, as expressing the love of God in terms of human love.[24] Scholars believe that Jewish writers had already allegorised the *Song*
by the time Christian writers took it up. By the mid-third
century the commentary of Origen (d. 254) was mainly responsible for the development of allegorical interpretation. Origen saw in it not just the union of Christ and the
church portrayed in terms of romantic love, but the mystical experience of the individual, of the soul seeking union
with God. With this view he combined the Gnostic attitude which, at its extreme, renounced human sexuality in
favour of mystical marriage, with a Platonic interpretation
of love, to transform the *Song* into a spiritual drama. At the
same time, he warned his readers not to think of it as in
any way to be about bodily actions, but to apply it to the
'apprehension of the divine senses of the inner man.'[25]

Gregory of Nyssa (d.394) wrote about the *Song* in the late fourth century in terms of union of the soul with God, and Jerome introduced this interpretation to the Western churches.[26] Much later some of the great mystics would take up this tradition – Bernard of Clairvaux, Teresa of Avila, John of the Cross. However, even in Patristic times there were a few dissenting voices – Theodore of Mopsuestia, and Jovinian, a monk – who understood the *Song* in its literal sense and who believed marriage was not an inferior state to virginity or celibacy. Both were condemned officially and Jerome, and later Augustine, wrote with what has been described as 'intense animosity' against Jovinian.[27]

It seems to me that the significant factor at this point may have been not so much who interpreted correctly, as that the weight of the 'official' church hijacked the only unadulterated praise of human sexual love that the *Song* is, and proposed a mystical marriage of the soul with God as the only acceptable reading of it. Nowhere do they say that ordinary human love and/or marriage is not good, but in using the *Song* to depict the mystical union of the soul with God, they robbed the interpersonal love of man and woman of its status as sacred, God-given gift in its own right. It seems to me that the split between the physical and the spiritual is false. The physical can be intrinsic to the mystical/spiritual as much in its being experienced to the full as in its being bypassed. If the ultimate expression of human love is mystical, as certain allegorisations of the *Song* suggest, then, by inference, the physical, albeit united with the spiritual, is at best less exalted and at worst an unhappy reminder of our lower nature and to be avoided by all who seek God. The question arises as to whether this unstated attitude to human love and sexuality (firmly in place well before Augustine), in forcing a split between the physical and the spiritual, has distorted the true place of human interpersonal love in the Christian tradition. The argument is not that the *Song* could not, or should not be allegorised, but rather that insistence on allegorisation as the only appropriate or possible reason for its inclusion in the canons of scripture has been a more powerful influence than any outright condemnation of sexual love as ungodly.

The allegorisations of Origen, of Gregory of Nyssa or Bernard of Clairvaux, of John of the Cross or Teresa, are certainly part of the story of the *Song* for us and to be treasured in our Christian tradition. But if the interpretation were to rest there, in the mystical realm, then access to the universal message of the *Song* about love is forever hijacked and taken out of the reach of ordinary lovers. This is not to take from the wonder of the mystical experience of the few, but it may be that their gain has been the loss of the wonder of ordinary human love to the many whose loving is in its way also particularly graced by God, and no less special for being bodily expressed.

It is this bodily expression, seen as separated from the spiritual in human persons, that greatly preoccupied Augustine who would exert the greatest influence on the Christian view of marriage up to the present time.[28]

AUGUSTINE

Of all the theologians in the history of the Western church, Augustine is credited with being the most influential with regard to marriage.[29] Many Christians would be aware of the generally accepted understanding of Augustine's notion of marriage as being for the procreation of children and an institution wherein sexual desire, passion, pleasure – all of which, in one interpretation of his view, are unworthy of the baptised and linked to original sin – may be contained if not quite controlled. What is sometimes overlooked is that the reason for his writing on marriage was to defend marriage and sexuality as goods, as part of God's plan for humanity, even if the plan in Augustine's view is somewhat or considerably awry.[30]

In the time of Augustine, marriage was being attacked

from two positions. One was that of the Manichean sect whose dualistic interpretation of the universe involved a rejection of marriage and sexual activity. This was counterbalanced by the view of Jovinian which held marriage and virginity to be of equal worth. The second source of attack was the accusation of the Pelagians, in particular Julian of Eclanum, that Augustine's notion of original sin, which led him to the belief that sexual intercourse was invariably sinful, in effect condemned marriage and sexuality as the Manicheans had done before him. In Julian's opinion this was compounded by Augustine's upholding the continent marriage of Joseph and Mary as a true marriage, even as the perfect marriage.[31]

As defence against the Manichees, Augustine wrote *De Bono Conjugali* in 401 AD. In this work he discusses marriage in terms of its three goods – children, fidelity and the sacrament.[32] Marriage cannot be evil when it is blessed with offspring, the fidelity of the husband and wife and the sacramental bond. In a later work, *De Nuptiis et Concupiscentia* (421), there is a clear exposition of his view on the effects of sin on sexuality and so on marriage. Augustine's great concern was with original sin and our need for grace to overcome its effects, which the Pelagians denied. He saw the inevitable contamination of all humans since the effects are handed on at conception through intercourse of the parents. It is not sexual intercourse itself that is evil in Augustine's view, since in Genesis 1:28 it is part of the Creation plan, but the accompanying non-rational elements, such as uncontrolled desire, passion, pleasure and so on, which are the effects of concupiscence and the result of original sin, making sexual activity almost inevitably sinful even within marriage.[33] The sin is lessened if the three goods are intended and pleasure in the act of intercourse itself is not a motivating factor. This obviously limits the legitimate expression of sexual love in marriage and it would only be a small step to seeing procreation as its only justification, since fidelity and the sacrament can exist without it. A possibly mitigating cause for intercourse would be in order that the spouse not commit adultery. Provided sexual union was suffered rather than sought, and any possible pleasure endured rather than enjoyed, it might be only venially sinful.

The above may seem to stress the more unbalanced aspects of Augustine's position. Has his view any redeeming features? This will be part of the topic of a later section. However, with such views controlling the approach to marriage in the West until the thirteenth century, perhaps it was not surprising that the original intention of upholding the goodness of marriage was somehow lost, and the conviction that virginity and celibacy are superior took firm hold. In fairness to Augustine, it should be remembered that he, like Paul, considered everything in the light of relationship to Christ. He had no hesitation in seeing the polygamy of the Old Testament patriarchs as equal in merit to the celibacy of Christians of his time, since both are for Christ.[34] He sees marriage and virginity as two goods, but the second is greater because of faith and the priorities that it gives rise to.[35] This position is still held by our church according to some theologians.[36] The goods of marriage of Augustine would be upheld and spoken of in terms of *primary* and *secondary* ends when taken over by Thomas Aquinas, which terminology would endure into the twentieth century.

THEOLOGY AND MARRIAGE IN THE MEDIEVAL PERIOD

The medieval period is characterised, on the one hand, by the theologians working towards the position where they can include marriage among the seven sacraments of the church and, on the other, by the canon lawyers working to a decision as to whether consent or consummation makes a marriage. The fruits of both were to be needed in the attempt to locate precisely the point at which a Christian marriage comes into being as sacrament and is therefore indissoluble.

Augustine had seen the character of marriage as sacrament as one of the three goods. However, it was not until the twelfth century that Peter Lombard listed marriage as a sacrament in the sense that we understand the seven sacraments of the church today.[37] He understood sacrament to be a sign of grace and also a cause of grace. There was doubt as to whether marriage was truly a sacrament. Could it be a cause of grace in view of its involving sex and in light of Augustine's teaching about it? It was finally Aquinas who stated that through the sacrament grace is given to the married. The Councils of Lyons 1274 and Florence 1439 listed marriage among the sacraments and specified that they contained grace and conferred it on those who received them worthily, respectively.[38]

What of the canon lawyers and their contribution to this period? The Christian church inherited marriage as a secular custom, the fundamental rules of which derived from Roman law. The intent to get married, consent, was what made marriage. In practice this was often consent of the parents rather than the couple, and divorce was easily available.[39] Marriage was as much about inheritance and the orderly transmission of property as it was about love and mutual giving. The involvement of the church in the law of marriage in Europe was gradual. The church aimed to establish monogamy for life as the norm of marriage, and the lay aristocracy and monarchs of Western Europe saw an advantage in monogamy to themselves, in that legitimate male heirs were most desirable.[40] At any rate the popes and bishops were drawn in to establish what breaches of canon law were involved in the complicated political and personal motives of certain monarchs for their various marriages.

As regards society generally, the main cause for the church gaining control over marriage between the seventh and twelfth centuries was that the stability of society required it. Marriage was marked by two abuses, clandestine marriages and very usual divorce, commonly on grounds of adultery. Both church and political leaders shared the need

to bring marriage under control – the church leaders to up-
hold Christian values and the political leaders to stabilise
society torn apart by the barbarian invasions.[41]

In 1215 the fourth Lateran Council proscribed clandestine
marriages and the focus for theologians and lawyers became consent and whether it was sufficient to make marriage. The canon lawyers at the University of Paris sup-
ported the notion that consent of the couple was what
made marriage. But children are of its essence, as the monarchs showed in their need for successors. However, the
canonists at Bologna took another view. For them marriage was made according to the Northern European tradition, by sexual intercourse *after* the exchange of consent.
Both sides of the debate had a basis in history and it was
Gratian, the Master at Bologna, who brought both elements to his solution in 1140. Known as Gratian's decree,
he proposed that consent initiates a marriage and legally
binds a couple but that subsequent sexual intercourse
completes it, makes a ratified and consummated marriage.
It is this marriage that is indissoluble, containing the three
goods of Augustine and yet upholding the virgin marriage
of Mary and Joseph.[42]

The canon lawyers now preoccupied themselves with the
relation between consent and consummation. The aim became to match the inner commitments of marriage to all
that was understood and implied at the time of consent,
the long term goals of fidelity, indissolubility and the procreation and upbringing of children.[43]

In due course, marriage that the church recognised as
sacramental and indissoluble was required to be celebrated
publicly in the presence of a priest and two witnesses. The
sixteenth century *Tametsi* decree of the Council of Trent
made marriage a solemn contract requiring certain legal
formalities for validity. As sacrament it is constituted by
the consent of the man and woman and is made indissoluble by their subsequent intercourse. The distinction of
Gratian between marriage *initiated*, which is valid but dis-

soluble, and marriage *consummated*, which is valid and indissoluble, and the prescribed form of Trent without which for Catholics marriage is neither valid nor a sacrament, entered into the canon law of the church and still decides disputed questions of legality, validity and sacramentality of marriages.[44] It would be several hundred years before Christian theology would consider the personal aspects of marriage.

In this second chapter the intention has been to show something of how marriage and the theology of marriage have interacted from early Christian times up to the time of new developments in the twentieth century.

Among the salient features of the tradition is the constant reiteration of the essential goodness of marriage and the equally constant reiteration of its indissolubility. The legacy of Augustine, the suspicion attached to sexuality and the human incapacity to entirely control it, which is still at the root of the ambivalence of many Christians towards sex today, dominated teaching on marriage for centuries. Nevertheless this was not sufficiently negative to prevent marriage being included among the sacraments of the church. A major positive contribution to the tradition was the *De Sacramentis Christianae Fidei* of Hugh of St Victor, composed about 1134, part eleven of which treats of marriage and is the basic work for the development of marriage as sacrament by Peter Lombard and later Aquinas.[45] This work is also the basis of the twelfth century decrees of Gratian and indeed contains all the fundamentals of church law concerning marriage up to the present time.

The organising of marriage formally is another positive feature of the Christian tradition of this period which culminated in the *Tametsi* decree of Trent. The development of canon law of marriage in terms of the identity of contract and sacrament, consent and consummation, was based on the theology of this period and would eventually be codified in 1917.

The question as to whether the marriage contract between

baptised persons is necessarily a sacrament and therefore indissoluble was, and continues to be, much debated among theologians. It is of particular importance today when so many people who are baptised have not the faith necessary for valid sacrament.

By the end of the medieval period, marriage is a contract and a sacrament. The uneasy attempt to reconcile the need to organise with the needs and hopes and aspirations, personal and religious and sometimes even political, of the members of the church, would continue in a primarily legalistic mode for a considerable period. The status quo with regard to marriage remained virtually unchanged from that time until the period prior to the Second Vatican Council which is the matter of the next chapter.

CHAPTER THREE

Main Trends in Modern Theology of Marriage

INTRODUCTION AND BACKGROUND TO VATICAN II

Modern theology of marriage is marked by two trends. Firstly theologians in the relatively recent past have chosen to consider marriage not primarily as institution, as was the case, but as a lived reality, a relationship of persons, with the recognition that men and women living their lives in this particular relationship have a contribution to make to the developing theology of marriage. This new emphasis on the experience of marriage as an important element in the discussion, particularly in the area of sexuality, finds expression in theological writing and indicates a refreshing realism and a sense of openness on the part of both clerical/religious and lay theologians. In general, recent theology does not see the married way of life as in any sense inferior to the celibate way, and there is a clear impression that, as marriage is a means of most people's way to God, the development of the theology of marriage is a task to be undertaken jointly.

The second significant trend is in the discussion of marriage as sacrament and concerns the question of indissolubility. Tradition, as reaffirmed in the 1983 *Code of Canon Law*, states that the marriage of two baptised persons is always a sacrament and as such is indissoluble.[1] Theologians of our time are faced with the reality of marriage breakdown on a scale not previously experienced, and the accompanying fact that many baptised persons are not believers in Christ or the church. There is an attempt to face these problems honestly, and questions of indissolubility and sacramentality as *givens* of Christian marriage, or as something *to be worked towards*, occupy much of the recent writing on marriage.

As indicated in the previous chapter, the teaching of the church on marriage from the time of Trent to the period leading up to the second Vatican Council was marked by its emphasis on the legal definition and requirements for the sacrament of marriage which found formal expression in the 1917 *Code of Canon Law*. Gasparri, the designer of the Code, had published a work in 1892 in which he presented marriage as a contract whose formal object is the permanent and exclusive mutual right of the spouses to one another's body for sexual intercourse and with procreation as primary over the other ends of marriage.[2] These notions were incorporated into the 1917 Code and the terms *primary* and *secondary* ends became central to discussions on marriage until Vatican II. As to what made marriage, Canon 1081.1 held that it was the consent of the parties legitimately expressed between persons capable of it by law. The development goes on in terms of rights (perpetual, exclusive), contracting parties, acts of themselves suitable for the generation of children, and so on. Marriage was seen as a binding, indissoluble contract, perhaps inevitable in what was a juridical context, but which, as a main source of theology of marriage, gave rise to an impoverished notion of the human reality and sacrament.

Where and in what way was the turning point to be observed? The 1930 encyclical of Pius XI, *Casti Connubii*, is considered to mark a new direction. In it the Pope reiterated the canonical position but went further in not only indicating the existence of mutual love at the heart of marriage but in stressing its importance.[3] This love aims at the mutual help and perfecting of the couple, so that through their partnership they may grow in true love towards God and their neighbour. This content of *Casti Connubii* is said to be one of the 'first major attempts on the part of the church to deal with married life and love as it unfolded after the wedding.'[4] The change from physicalist, natural law categories to a view of husband and wife as spiritual persons was taken up by two German writers, Von Hildebrand and Doms, both influenced by the personalist philosophy of their time. Von Hildebrand claimed conjugal love and community as the 'ultimate and primary meaning' of marriage. He argued that the fusion of their very beings is what is intended by the 'one body' of Genesis and that sexual intercourse achieves its primary end when it leads to this.[5] Doms went a stage further in pointing out that human sexuality is of a different order to animal biology and drives persons to give their whole self to the other and to accept the gift of the other as person. For Doms, the meaning of intercourse is the giving and accepting that leads to the union of the couple. Although conception and the birth of children is the natural fruit of this love, what he calls the immediate purpose of the marriage – the two-in-oneness – is a purpose in itself and achieved even in childless marriages.[6] It is *union* that is the source of well-being of husband and wife and the means to achieving the other ends. The position of Doms and others was condemned by decree of the Congregation of the Holy Office in 1944, but the challenge continued and Pius XII reaffirmed the 1944 decree in October 1951 in an address to obstetricians. In this he subordinated all meaning, purpose and ends of marriage to procreation. According to one contemporary theologian, Theodore Mackin, in this presentation 'not only does marriage exist first and principally for procreation and nurture but everything else of value in it is for them. The spouses' love for one another is there for the sake of the offspring; their striving for maturity as husband and wife is for offspring'.[7]

The debate about the hierarchy of ends in marriage and the relative value of the love of husband and wife and the procreation of children, continued up to and into the Second Vatican Council.

VATICAN II: GAUDIUM ET SPES

The problem of disputed primary/secondary ends and the values therein was the main concern of the council fathers in their treatment of the sacrament of marriage. The outcome was presented in the second part of *The Pastoral Constitution on the Church in the Modern World* (*Gaudium et Spes*) (1965). Marriage here is described as 'a community of love' and as 'an intimate partnership of conjugal life and love' based in a 'conjugal covenant of irrevocable personal consent' (n. 48).[8] The change in terminology from contract to covenant symbolises powerfully the profound change in attitude that views marriage as a personal reality, one that recalls the Old Testament covenant of Yahweh with his people Israel and the New Testament covenant of Christ and the church. The personal is further emphasised in the statement that husband and wife 'mutually gift and accept one another'. The impoverished notion implied in talk of rights over one another's bodies is replaced by that of the mutual gifting of persons which creates a new, permanent reality. The institution of marriage and the love of husband and wife are 'by their nature ordained to the generation and education of children', but this 'does not make the other purposes of marriage of less account' (n. 50). Marriage is no longer described in terms of primary and secondary ends; the love and life together of husband and wife and the procreating of children are presented as equally important.

In *Humanae Vitae*, the encyclical of Paul VI on The Regulation of Birth (1968), marriage is presented as 'ordered to the wellbeing of the spouses and to the procreation and upbringing of children'. How seriously this new position was to be taken is illustrated by the fact that in the 1983 *Code of Canon Law* the word *contract* has been replaced by *covenant*. Marriage is brought into being by consent, which is an 'act of the will by which a man and a woman, by irrevocable covenant, mutually give and accept one another for the purpose of establishing a marriage' (Canon 1057.2).[9]

The theology of marriage has influenced the law of the church to the extent of including the personal realities of marriage in its description, and this in turn would have major implications for the decisions of tribunals and for the further development of theology.

RAHNER: A BRIDGE BETWEEN VATICAN II AND MODERN THEOLOGY

In the decades preceding Vatican II, the most notable contribution to theology of marriage was made by Edward Schillebeeckx, who worked to interpret the place of marital love in the sacrament.[10] For almost a century, resistance to the secularisation of marriage, accompanied by the assertion that Christian marriage is always sacramental, was based mainly on the work of a German, Mathias Scheeben.[11] He held all marriages to be natural sacraments, and Christians, because of their baptism with its special character which incorporates them into the Mystical Body of Christ, marry as members of Christ's body and their marriage cannot but be Christian sacrament. Theodore Mackin goes so far as to suggest that Scheeben, in using the marriage passage in Ephesians 5:21-33 as the basis for his understanding of the sacramentality of marriage, makes the Pauline metaphor the reality itself of the sacramental marriage. The Christian marriage is not just an image of the union of Christ and the church, but is 'rooted in this mystery and is organically connected with it and so partakes of its nature and mysterious character'.[12]

Schillebeeckx was to develop this notion of marriage as sacrament in the context of christology. Christ is God's primary sacrament. Baptism joins Christians to God's saving work in Christ. When Christians marry they co-operate in this work specifically as married, and their part in it, both physical and spiritual, becomes sacramental. Schillebeeckx argues indissolubility, not from the unbreakable Christ/church relationship, but ultimately from the irrevocability of the spouses' consent, which derives from their baptism. Because they are baptised they make their commitment in the power of Christ's commitment. Later, in an essay written in 1974 and translated in 1975 entitled 'Christian Marriage and the Human Reality of Complete Marital Disintegration', he maintains that indissolubility is not a *given* but is *to be attained* in marriage by the spouses' effort to love one another resolutely, by their joining of their wills to Christ's will to make their marriage a sacrament.[13] Schillebeeckx, with this developed view of indissolubility, illustrates the effect of the change from considering marriage in the abstract as sacramental to looking at sacramentality in the lived relationship of spouses.

In this context, Christian marriage as lived relationship, the contribution of Karl Rahner in his 1967 article 'Marriage as Sacrament',[14] could be seen as both grounding the apparently new theology of the council documents and, at the same time, providing a springboard for some of the main developments of the eighties. In the sacrament, human action and the saving will of God meet in the symbolic ritual. The sacrament is one means of the church actualising itself: the grace offered and accepted in freedom in the sacrament can bring about a unity between what is the sign and what is the reality – Christian marriage is a sign of the unity of Christ and the church. The living of the sacrament by the married is one way in which the unifying love of the church is made actual.

Perhaps more significant still in Rahner's writing is his treatment of the personal love at the heart of the marriage relationship, which he believes should be considered 'in its own distinctive nature'.[15] He sees marriage as a sign of personal love at the physical and social level before it is a sacrament. In his understanding of this love of husband and wife for one another (in all its aspects) as from, of and oriented to God, as acquiring fresh roots through grace and as uniting the whole of humanity, I believe Rahner overcomes the physical/spiritual divide that is so characteristic of talk of love in our Christian tradition, and frees theologians, and so the married also, to consider this love in new ways.

Rahner sees love of God and love of neighbour as mutually conditioning one another. Creation is God's self-communication and, for Rahner, God is primarily recognisable in personal interrelationships. Because it is God's love that animates and sustains creation, gives humans life and love, and draws all to God through it, then the love between two people can lead them to reach one another in the deepest level of their being. The personal love which manifests itself in marriage is, through its source in the love of God, salvific, and intends God not only in the transcendent but in the nearness in which God's self is revealed – as the innermost mystery and life of the human person.

In addressing the relationship of married love to humanity in general, Rahner poses some pertinent questions. Where does the exclusiveness in relation to others, characteristic of married love, come from? Is it of the nature of personal love, or are there other less basic reasons to do with the concrete physical manifestations of this love, as these are limited by space and time? Are there cultural, social and sociological factors determining this exclusiveness? Marriage, for Rahner, is not a 'we' set apart from the 'all', but a 'we' open to all. People come from a community, their love becomes fruitful in the child, who must be free to become part of the community of the 'all'. Married love is a source of, and initiation into, a wider community. It involves the task to love humanity in itself, to be ready to trust the other again and again with the self, and to commit the whole of oneself to the other. The same grace – God's self-communication – that sustains married love and opens it to God, is also that which unites the individual to all others. In this human love, which is at once love of God, there is the possibility to reach beyond the self, and, united by it to all humanity, to go with the basic thrust of all people towards unity in God.

With regard to the sacramentality of marriage, Rahner asserts that what is said of marriage can also be said of the church. The church is the basic sacrament. What unites the couple is love animated by God's grace: both are signs; their union is a sacrament because it makes evident God's saving love at work in the church. For Rahner, there is no need to look to Ephesians 5 to support the sacramental status of marriage. Marriage is already an event of grace and becomes a sacramental event of grace when it is completed by baptised persons in the church. God created all human persons to call them to himself, this by means of his covenant, and the meeting point is Christ. In Christian marriage, spouses are joined in covenantal love. As church, married people help to sustain the human side of the relationship of God and church and in this their marriage is a sacrament.

The significance of Rahner's contribution to the theology of marriage is based in his belief that all of creation is graced – animated by God's own self-communication. All human love, therefore, in so far as it is a going out of self and a reaching towards another, is a reaching for God, and even a making present of God's love in our world. The love of married people, in all of its particular manifestations, is included in Rahner's understanding. This amounts to a virtual rehabilitation of sexual love as also belonging in God's love and being of itself sacramental. It is this aspect that I think theologians writing in the eighties were freed to take up and pursue in a way not previously possible. No longer is there the need to justify sexual love in marriage. Although Rahner assumes children to be the natural fruit of this love, he does not suggest that this is its purpose. Indeed it is not for anything more important than drawing humans to their creator and to one another. The most welcome aspect of Rahner's understanding is that love need not be split into categories, that God is present in all love. It may be that future theologians will return again and again to Rahner in trying to come to the truth of love in the many human relationships that are not marriage and are yet waiting to be included in the human view of God's saving love.

PERSONAL LOVE IN THEOLOGIANS FOLLOWING RAHNER

How did the notion of the personal love at the heart of marriage develop among the theologians interpreting the change of emphasis in Rahner and Vatican II? Walter Kasper, in *Theology of Christian Marriage* (original German text published 1977), recognises the need for theology to develop a more precise understanding of the human values in marriage. Like Rahner, he sees humans as seeking and finding fulfillment through relationship, so that in the marriage relationship there is a love that unites intimately while yet setting free to independent personal existence. This love is understood as personal, fruitful and faithful, and he sees sexuality, which permeates the entire being of the human person, and so is central to our expression and communication, as needing to be integrated into personal bonds to be realised humanly. Since marriage involves the whole person of both partners, he considers it the most meaningful place for full sexual expression. Like Mackin and Dominian, Kasper emphasises the healing part played by marriage in integrating sex and eroticism into the whole human and religious structure of the individual and society. He would see the sacramentality of marriage here, in that it is a representation and making effective of the redemptive work of God in its healing of the disintegration and fragmentation of human existence due to sin.

An important feature of Kasper's theology is his explicit recognition that love includes justice: love accepts but also gives the other his or her due. He does not develop the theme beyond saying that marriage is an institutional reality affected by the social and economic conditions in which it is lived, and that the balance between the personal and institutional needs to be maintained. However, his including of justice as of the essence of love in marriage is relatively unique and perhaps even prophetic, given the way the perception of marriage changed as the feminist movement grew in significance subsequently. A second important aspect in Kasper is his understanding of the fruitfulness of love in marriage as having more than a biological meaning. Like Rahner, he assumes children to be the natural desired outcome of love in marriage, but sees a much wider connotation to the outward thrust of this love.

If Kasper is somewhat tentative in his discussion of the sexual in married love, Mackin, Dominian, and Michael Lawler are precisely the opposite.[16] All of them see sexual intercourse between husband and wife as of itself the core of the sacramentality of marriage, and this independently of its likely, or probable, or desired outcome in the birth of children.

Mackin's starting point, like that of Rahner, is the love of God for humanity which is at once creative and redemptive. The humanity of Christ is God's means of drawing people to him, of overcoming sin, which resists his reason for our existence and defeats our efforts at relationships of trust and love. Mackin suggests that fear of the loss of self may be at the root of our incapacity to love as the Creator intended. Maybe this fear is our original sin. He shares with Kasper, and to an even more emphatic degree with Dominian, that marriage as sacrament within the church sacrament, and specifically the sexual love at its heart, is a specific means for this healing.

Affirming the progress in understanding of the personal relationship as covenantal in *Gaudium et Spes* of Vatican II, Mackin is never the less critical of its falling short in understanding the place of sexuality in marriage and in the matrix of the sacrament. Engaging in sexual love is for Christian spouses at the same time the living of the sacrament. He believes the fullest expression of their love is in sexual lovemaking and right there is Christ present to them. Is all married lovemaking then sacramental and holy? Not so, according to Mackin. Sexuality, in this context, includes the desire for emotional interpenetration, the wanting to know the partner completely and to be completely known. He points out that to love sexually demands the capacity and willingness to take down barriers to this emotional interpenetration. The need and will to hold one's partner at an emotional distance in order to guard the self may be what sin *is* in context of sexuality.

The significance of sexual love in marriage, as giving life to the couple, cannot be overstated in the view of Jack Dominian.[17] He would model the family interacting in and through love on the Trinity, as persons interacting with each other in and through love. He sees marriage in terms of sustaining, healing and growth for the couple, and permanence as necessary for this. In his work, *Passionate and Compassionate Love*, he is more explicit in discussing the meaning of sexual intercourse in marriage. Dominian calls sexual intercourse 'a body language of love'.[18] What does he think this language communicates? In sexual intercourse the couple affirm the personhood and sexual identity of each other. His evidence shows that, after conflict of long or short duration, after pain and hurt of greater or lesser degree, it is sexual intercourse that brings reconciliation. He sees intercourse as an act of recurrent hope and celebration of meaning in life and as a recurrent act of thanksgiving for life itself. As related to the metaphor of Paul, the relationship of Christ and the church, Dominian sees sexual intercourse as 'the central and recurrent act of prayer of the couple.'[19] Is this very different from what Rahner has said?

The place of sexuality and of sexual intercourse in Christian marriage, unity at the physical, psychological and spiritual level, as well as the pressing question of faith and sacrament (which will be treated later in the chapter), are concerns of Michael Lawler.[20] He shares many of the psychological insights of Kasper, Mackin and Dominian, but with more of an emphasis on the 'two in one body' as image of the unity of Christ and the church than the others. Manifesting the covenant love of Christ and the church is not a given of marriage, says Lawler, in common with the later Schillebeeckx, but a project that must take a lifetime to complete. Unity is not a blending of persons but rather an accepting and valuing of the self and partner at all levels.

Where Mackin sees fear of the loss of self, Lawler sees self-ishness and the desire to control the other as what is most likely to threaten the achievement of unity and produce an inadequate symbol of the unity of Christ and the church.

Because of the traditional ambivalence of Christianity towards sexuality, Lawler indulges in what he calls 'reverse discrimination' in this regard.[21] For many Christians, married or unmarried, acceptance of their gift of sexuality is more difficult than its restraint. The tendency he perceives in modern Catholic theology to spiritualise sexuality and intercourse, (in an effort to make it acceptable?),[22] seeing sexual intercourse exclusively in terms of encounter, communicating, expressing love and so on, is as problematic for him as treating it only on the physical level. He is convinced that the traditional distrust of physical expression of sexuality needs to be redressed. To become one body spouses must come to terms with their individual and mutual needs, feelings and desires on the physical, psychological and spiritual levels. Married love is never exclusively selfish love but it is in part selfish love. It is loving your neighbour as yourself. In a marriage where each person is a full partner, together and as individuals the spouses love each and both as one.

What of the place of sexual desire in marriage? Are sexual passion and pleasure, treated so circumspectly, with wariness and even negative suspicion in the tradition, to be included in our understanding of Christian marriage as sacrament, as place of God's encounter with men and women? Can such expressions and effects of the man/woman relationship really be a means to holiness, a way in which God draws people to himself? Emphatically yes, according to Mackin and Lawler, whose treatment of them distinguishes these theologians from most other writers on marriage.[23] In Lawler sexuality, sexual passion and pleasure are God's good gifts to humanity: to use them in becoming one in marriage is to do so in a way that points to their source in God, a use that is human, Christian and graceful. Further, the more heightened and sharply focused are sexual passion and sexual pleasure the more they achieve their nature, the more God's gift is valued and the giver may be praised. Lawler turns to the *Song of Songs*, in which it is precisely the physical union of the lovers which has an important place in symbolising the covenant love between God and humanity. The love expressed in the *Song* is explicitly passionate, erotic love; the whole being of the lovers is centred in delight and desire for one another; to be sick with love, with passion, with desire, this is the love that men and women know for, in, and through one another and which leads them to seek the bodily presence of the other. In the exchange that is sexual intercourse, the gift of love is celebrated and here the creator God and God's love for humanity are simultaneously celebrated. It is Lawler's contention that human sexual passion and pleasure have much in them that is non-rational, and that people become fully human by accepting this joyfully and integrating it into their lives.

On the same topic, Mackin has a different perspective. He sees the human desire for the perfection of goodness and beauty as the basis of sexual passion. Passion is the emotional energy that drives men and women to search for them, 'to produce them in great art and in ardent love'.[24] Passion, in one Christian interpretation, is understood as an implicit desire for union with God, a desire by which he draws men and women to himself. How do people reach to an attraction to God by locking their passion in the following of the goodness and beauty of a man or woman? Where is God to be found and experienced in physical and emotional communion with a human being? Here Rahner's love of God through love of neighbour is aptly illustrated; the transcendence that is involved in this particular human relationship can be precisely an entry into the divine/human relationship. If partners are to be fulfilled in the sexual expression of passion, they must be physically and emotionally penetrable. Is it in this risk-all situation, the nakedness of soul and body, all barriers to intimacy removed, this place of trust without reserve, that God may be found? Is it in the loosing of passion on one another that arouses and intensifies desire and opens the partners to such joy?

The place of sexual pleasure in the sacrament of marriage is identified by Mackin as in intensifying happiness in one's partner in the most complete way. In the physical and emotional interpenetration, in the psychological joining and completion, there is an essential giving and accepting. Part of the pleasure one gives is the accepting of the pleasure-giving of the other. If holiness is union with God and, in the context of our world, it is working with God to heal the sinfulness in us, then it follows for Mackin that to be open to the draw and experience of pleasure that leads to a removal of barriers to intimacy, makes for trust, increases desire, that impels one to do this for a loved partner, is to open oneself to God. In Christian marriage, to co-work with God through sexuality, as described by Mackin, is to carry out ministry that is sacramental.

MARRIAGE AS SACRAMENTALLY INDISSOLUBLE

The development in the teaching on marriage of Vatican II stimulated theological and pastoral renewal and was also the cause of debate. There were many questions that needed reflection, clarification and answers. In 1977 the International Theological Commission, a group of Catholic theologians appointed by the Holy See, set themselves the task of addressing five problem areas: 1) Marriage as Institution; 2) Marriage as Sacrament; 3) Marriage as contract/covenant as it relates to marriage as sacrament; 4) Indissolubility; 5) Remarriage. The findings of the Commission were published in English in 1977 and the work comprises a collection of concluding statements, the position papers, and auxiliary studies prepared by the Commission. The theological reflection of the group shows a preoccupation with the question of the identity of contract and sacrament and the matter of indissolubility of marriages.[25] The work shows an awareness of the reality of the problems of marriage and of faith at the latter part of the twentieth century. The format is a statement of propositions about marriage, followed by papers on various aspects with some responses. Among the propositions are – marriage is a sacrament, confers grace through Christ and not just through faith of the receiver but presupposes and demands faith at least to a minimal degree; marriage for the baptised is always a sacrament; marriage is indissoluble; the divorced who have remarried may not take full part in the eucharist unless through penance and the renouncing of sexual relations.

The above in a way belies the content of the papers and yet it must be said that all the new understanding and awareness of the human person and of marriage as persons in relationship, of the profound changes in the societies and cultures of our time, has not led to change in regard to the institutional aspects of marriage in the church as far as the magisterium is concerned. However the effects of accepting personal love as the main motive for marriage has given rise to questions about the perceived rigidity of Catholic teaching about marriage and the exercise of sexuality in the variety of relationships that do not constitute marriage. Principally this refers to the question as to whether the bond of marriage can be said to exist when the love on which it is said to be based ceases to exist. Questions about indissolubility, tensions between the interpersonal and institutional dimensions of marriage, the lack of understanding on the part of people and priests of some juridical positions with regard to nullity and the scandal it sometimes occasions, are all observed openly, and the Commission is reminded that law and legislation must keep in mind the service of human and Christian reality.[26]

The importance attributed to sexuality in marriage is noted and there is a caution against hedonism. Noted too is the 'discontent, incomprehension, rejection' encountered in the face of the teaching that sexual relations are reserved exclusively for marriage and the fact of the absence of guilt in this matter even among those who continue to avail of the sacrament of reconciliation. The notion of trial marriages is firmly rejected alongside the affirmation that pastoral directives are necessary to meet concrete needs in this area. The uncertainty in theology in the area of indissolubility is noted and there is an understanding of the difficulty in accepting current church discipline that tolerates the common life of a union after divorce but requires that sexual intercourse be excluded. Wilhelm Ernst refers to the right of the church to look again at scripture and its own teaching in the light of the faith of the time, as instanced in the past by the broadening of the Pauline and Petrine privileges and the distinction between indissoluble sacramental marriages and marriages that can sometimes be dissolved. In the area of law he points to theological, social and psychological difficulties which need to be addressed in a revision of canon law which would adequately cater for the relationship between the personal, and institutional and juridical dimensions of marriage, which express a tension but not an opposition.

The matter of sacramentality and indissolubility occupy both Karl Lehmann and Carlo Caffarra although each writes with a different emphasis.[27] Nature and grace, creation and covenant are fundamentally linked for the Christian and indissolubility and sacramentality are inevitable from the nature of baptism and the wholeness of the human person, according to Lehmann. Unlike Schillebeeckx, he sees indissolubility as both a given and a task for the spouses. In discussing faith and baptism as the basis of the sacrament, Lehmann implicitly admits the possibility of a contradiction between sacramental theology and canon law as it presently stands.[28] He accepts that theologians have differed as to the separability of contract and sacrament and that in our time faith and intention, validity and fruitfulness of the sacrament are questions preoccupying those involved in marriage pastorally. However the existential incorporation into the Body of Christ that baptism involves means in Lehmann's view that two baptised persons contracting a marriage are not entitled to decide on their own what their union is to mean.

Caffarra takes this discussion a stage further and concludes that since marriage is instituted for the sake of the covenant with God in Christ, and through the gift of the Spirit, only sacramental marriage is possible for the baptised. He recognises that the problem of the relationship between nature and grace is at the centre of a new theological debate, but is adamant that no marriage is the result of baptised persons attempting to marry non-sacramentally.[29] With clear reference to the French diocese of Autun, and the attempt there to deal with the problem of lack of faith among the baptised by way of a 'welcomed' civil marriage in place of a sacramental marriage (with the hope of opening the couple to the sacrament at a later stage), Caffarra states that alternatives are confusing to the minds of Christians. In fact he considers alternatives to be intrinsically misrepresentative of the position of the church.

Caffarra's position is more closed than that of Lehmann and would seem to put those pastorally involved in an impossible situation, with regard to the sacrament and the baptised unbeliever. The real situation is not well addressed by either theologian. Lehmann does point out that indissolubility is contracted through consent and sees consummation as more than merely physical. (This is an important shift in 'official' treatment of consummation.) He recognises that the intimate sharing of life is what gives its integral meaning to sexual intimacy and that it is here that conjugal consent is verified, sealed and comes to fruition. The real symbolism of the union of Christ and the church is located in the sexual union of the couple seen as fulfillment and integration of the community of life. Christian marriage participates in that union in its most intimate reality. This grounds indissolubility and fundamentally distinguishes the marriage of the baptised from that of the unbeliever.

The theme of nature and grace in Vatican II is the matter of a response to Caffarra's paper, by Philippe Delhaye.[30] He situates the relation of nature and grace within the framework of salvation history. Creation and salvation together are the plan of God for humanity. Delhaye points out that in hypothesising pure nature in the sixteenth century, theologians wanted to emphasise the gratuity of the supernatural. However, there was a negative aspect in that theological thinking developed within the perspective of nature, natural law theory, morality and so on. He believes the consequences for marriage were grave since the starting point was marriage on the hypothetical level of philosophical nature. Vatican II attempted to redress the balance, not doing away with the distinction between nature and grace but expressing the distinction and co-ordination of the two orders – creation and redemption – and placing both within the perspective of salvation history. There is one end, participation in the life of God, and, in view of this, humanisation is both a means to an end and the result of grace. The 'autonomy of earthly realities' of Vatican II applies also to marriage but, according to Delhaye, recent attempts to place it outside the sacrament falsify the reality. Delhaye seems to be saying directly to Caffarra that he is mistaken, that all marriage is naturally sacramental – this may imply that baptised persons who marry without the church do marry validly and, in common with all married couples, image the covenant between God and humanity. The debate must continue.

Familiaris Consortio,
SOME RESPONSES TO IT, AND OTHER APPROACHES

The exhortation *Familiaris Consortio* of John Paul II (1981), on the role of the Christian family, includes much of the content of the papers of the International Theological Commission and, in particular, acceptance of the propositions enunciated by the Commission. The explicit recognition of the equal dignity of women with men in society and in marriage (n. 23) marks the beginning of the redressing of the balance in the Catholic view of women's place in family and society. The consideration of the role of men as husbands and fathers (n. 25), family as community of persons (n. 22), and the relationship of husband and wife as 'a very special form of friendship' (n. 25), are among the very positive elements in this treatment of family and society. The statements about pastoral care of people in 'certain irregular situations' (n. 79-85), reflect awareness of much of the reality of life at the end of the twentieth century, already attested to by the Commission.

How have some women theologians responded to this recent teaching and to broader issues about marriage and family? Lisa Sowle Cahill, in *Community and Couple: Marital Commitment*,[31] welcomes several aspects such as its egalitarian tone, personalist philosophy, and interpretation of sexuality as including physical and spiritual dimensions in interaction with one another. She is none the less critical of the use of biblical evidence to support traditional theological and moral positions, suggesting that the teaching about marriage and family is still not based on the real experience of married people. As an example Cahill queries whether the biblical ideal of Genesis 1 and 2, at the basis of the Pope's teaching on the 'nuptial' significance of the body, really yields the norm that every authentically loving sexual union will also be procreative. The teaching of Paul VI (*Humanae Vitae*) is reiterated in n. 32, where the Pope describes contraception as leading to a 'falsification of the inner truth of conjugal love'. Cahill here calls for more serious dialogue with married persons about the relationship of having children to their conjugal commitment and to their sex lives.

With regard to the role of women, Cahill maintains there is still ambivalence, the maternal and family role being given recognition more than all others. Theoretically, equality between the sexes is endorsed but, practically, the conditions and consequences of true effective equality are not followed out or even recognised. For example, Cahill points out that the Pope links 'the equal dignity and responsibility of women with men' to 'reciprocal self-giving' in marriage and family (n. 22). He claims too that 'women's access to public functions' is 'fully' justified. Yet there is ambivalence in the qualification which follows it: 'On the other hand, the true advancement of women requires that clear recognition be given to the value of their maternal and family role, by comparison with all other public roles and all other professions' (n. 23). The role of the father is 'of unique and irreplacable importance' (n. 25). The father is called on to share the development and education of their children with his wife, but this is not contrasted with the importance of his other roles, nor, as Cahill points out, is it explicitly suggested that the father share in the 'less elevated duties associated with the daily routines of childcare and household maintenance'.[32] She asks the pertinent question as to how the description of a genuine male-female love relationship as one of 'mutual self-gift' can be accurate if equal social resources in support of the personal freedom and marital and parental commitment of both partners do not exist. She draws on other women theologians to emphasise the need to set marriage within the context of social conditions and responsibilities – the success of a marriage is crucially related to factors beyond the intentional commitment of the partners as such,[33] and certain forms of social support for the family as a unit and for all its members are required.

Cahill is critical of Catholic teaching that portrays marriage in idealised terms and of the focus on sexual intercourse as the epitome of the spousal partnership. She is sympathetic to the view of theologians who interpret marital intimacy as cyclical, and who, unlike Mackin and Lawler, resist the temptation to see sexual acts as the occasions on which the relationship as a whole is at its peak moments.

Noting that successful upbringing of children requires more than generosity and the commitment of parents, Cahill is mindful of the fact that in all areas of marital commitment many existential situations are 'compromises with, or adjustments to, pre-existing factors which are less than ideal'. While not capitulating to relativism she does indicate that diverse and often complex experiential situations challenge our attempt to capture their reality with categories induced from other, albeit similar, experiences. The commitment of the Catholic tradition to seeking out objectivity and shared values must go on with the recognition that 'objectivity' and 'values' are revealed and made real in and through the lives of many individuals, relations, and communities.[34]

Rosemary Haughton, like Cahill, is also critical of a reworking of old theology into patterns more acceptable to the new consciousness as insufficient, and she proposes an openness to a theology of marriage which emerges from, and reflects, the new consciousness of men and women. Her stance comes from her working and living with women whose experience has often belied the teaching and ideal presentation of marriage by both church and society. 'A theology of marriage shattered by experience' is a dramatic description of the traditionally held theology.[35] She considers women whose moment of conversion has been the decision to seek divorce.

Like Cahill, and quite unlike any of the male theologians, Haughton asserts that the realities that now exist in the area of sex relations cannot be interpreted in terms of traditional theology of marriage. She believes that single parent families, unmarried or divorced women living together and bringing up children as one household, homosexual or lesbian couples doing likewise, call for new understanding. The friendships, intimacy, sexual relationships that develop and the moral status attributed to them, are all to be looked at in theological terms if it is in the giving and receiving of life and love that God's presence is to be discerned. Haughton poses an interesting question in the context of physical intimacy in a variety of relationships – at what point and on what grounds does God suddenly cease to be present? By this circuitous route she comes to the question about what happens between happily married people, and concludes friendship as the basic relationship, friendship involving fidelity and commitment, friendship that was offered to disciples in the New Testament in return for the family ties they broke. As friends they were to love and serve one another, not to dominate. Haughton believes this category of friendship to be rooted in the gospel and that it will serve as a basis for looking at relationships in categories other than sexual or legal. The strength of Haughton's contribution is in looking at how things *are*, and putting this in historical context, in addressing the gospel possibility of existential relationships of women and men in our time, and in openly considering their implications for the future.

If the work of Haughton and others is to deal with varieties of relationship after or without marriage, it is that of Kevin Kelly to attempt to provide some solutions to the basic problem of broken marriages and subsequent relationships within the church.[36] Kelly believes marriage as truly human demands indissolubility, but, like Schillebeeckx and Lawler, he is of the opinion that it must be brought into being within the marriage itself. It is a task to be undertaken. Like Lehmann, Dominian and others, he examines the meaning of consummation – a key factor in the indissolubility of sacramental marriages – and concludes it to be about persons becoming one in that they experience themselves as couple.

Can a marriage cease to exist? Does the bond exist independently of the couple? Kelly says that if the heart of marriage exists in the personal relationship of life-giving love, when this relationship ceases to exist the matter of the sacrament no longer exists, and the sacrament of marriage has ceased to exist. What of marriage after divorce? The constant teaching of the church is that sacrament cannot be separated from the human reality, so if a marriage after divorce is accepted as a real marriage, (as Delhaye seemed to argue that it should, on grounds of natural sacramentality of all marriage) then it must be sacramental in some sense. Sacraments can be effective in varying degrees. As public sign or as lived experience a second marriage is impaired as a sign of fidelity, and for Kelly, though sacramental, is not to be on a par with the first marriage from the sacramental point of view.

Kelly believes that the theological arguments for excluding the divorced and remarried from communion at the eucharist are not well founded. He cites *Familiaris Consortio* n. 84 as recognising that, while objectively contradicting the union of love between Christ and the church, the fact that they are to be encouraged to be actively involved in all aspects of the life of the church is not consistent with a judgment that a couple is living in a personal stance of mortal sin. He admits to having changed his stance on the necessity of their exclusion, and deals with the eucharist as sign of already existing community *vis à vis* eucharist as help to achieve unity. He appears to favour the action of the Eastern church, where remarriage is permitted but not regarded as the same as a first marriage, and where there is a penitential element involved in recognising sin in the failure of the first marriage.[37]

Kelly looks at the question of responsible dissent and judges that there may be conditions under which a Catholic in a second marriage after divorce would be making a fully responsible decision in presenting for Holy Communion. The tension between what is public proclamation and what is pastoral practice is at the centre of the problem. Kelly affirms his faith in marriage as indissoluble, but he lives in the real world of irretrievable breakdown of individual marriages. His own pain and compassion are transparent – his problem is the problem of the whole church.

Lest the impression be given here that all modern theology of marriage is in the spirit of *Gaudium et Spes* of Vatican II, mention must be made of a recent work carrying the official *imprimatur* of the Pontifical Council for the Family in Rome. *What God Has Joined: The Sacramentality of Marriage* is the contribution of Peter Elliott to modern theology of marriage. Elliott's main emphasis is on marriage as part of the 'great mystery'. He presents strongly traditional views on 'the inseparable foes of marriage, abortion, sterilisation and contraception.'[38] Contraception is an 'attack on the primary, natural, good of procreation', 'the divine economy' is 'inscribed in the fruitfulness of each woman'. Elliott seeks 'to rediscover the meaning of the unchanged teaching of the magisterium on the higher value of virginity' (p. 160). Developments in theology of marriage in Vatican II and changes in the status and role of women in marriage are minimally represented. The whole is placed in the context of marriage as image of the Christ/church relationship, this in common with other theologians such as Schillebeeckx, but uniquely with continuous use of mystical sexual language to describe this.

This very recent theology gives rise to some questions. Is the emphasis on marriage as part of the 'great mystery', to the virtual exclusion of much of the reality of people's lives at the end of the twentieth century, likely to prove helpful to those struggling with real marriages, whether existentially or pastorally? Would the effect of proposing a kind of mystical sexuality be inevitably to downgrade the sexuality of most ordinary people? Could the whole give the impression that much of the development of Vatican II, what some would see as progress, far from being Spirit-inspired was more in the nature of an aberration and needs to be set right? Are ordinary marriages to be measured against the yardstick of the very exceptional mystical union described in the poetry of St John of the Cross? Would it be healthy for Christian marriage in general if they were?

Elliott's reference throughout to baptism implies that many of the problems surrounding the sacramentality of marriage are based on a poor understanding of the first sacrament, and, in common with other theologians, he stresses the need for work in this area and for increased help for those about to be married, as well as support for the married.

CONCLUSION

In this chapter the attempt has been to give a general overview of recent theology of marriage. It reflects, on the one hand, the unchanged position regarding sacramentality and indissolubility on the part of the magisterium as stated in the propositions of the International Theological Commission, confirmed by *Familiaris Consortio*, and, on the other, the vastly altered and sometimes conflicting positions of theologians reflecting on the sacrament and on the lived reality of marriage. The strongly stated position of Caffarra, for example, is illustrative of the continued identification of contract and sacrament, and yet the inclusion of Delhaye's response seems to leave the way open for further reflection in the short term, and must lead to development in the area of indissolubility. That Lehmann should reiterate that consent and consummation make marriage indissoluble and then go on to open the meaning of consummation in personal terms must indicate that this will be an area for reflection and development. The awareness of the problem of the scale of marriage breakdown, and of its generally damaging effects on persons, is common to all. Locating the source of the situation in the regions of faith, personal expectations, the tension between the private and public dimensions of marriage, as well as the good and hopeful developments and changes in lived marriages, is reflected in varying degrees by the theologians. Marriage as sacrament in the church, as a source of grace, as a means to holiness, as an effective participation in the love that is Christ's for the church, is being given or restored its status in modern theology as a created and redeemed reality, willed by God, as one way of sharing in God's life that is love.

If the reference to personal love in marriage in the Vatican

II documents is somewhat tentative, perhaps because of its being a new departure in such writing, the treatment by Rahner, Mackin and others is precisely the opposite. That all love is from and directed to God, and relates humans to God and to one another, may seem to have little to do with married love as commonly understood. Yet it is exactly this that married people need to be reminded of in a culture where the very exclusiveness thought to sustain marriage seems to have reached destructive proportions and is surely an important factor in marriage breakdown. Love between married people is, of course, exclusive in a certain sense and sometimes properly inward looking, but this is not all. It is also a means of the couple's reaching out to, and being connected with, the wider community. Rahner's clear statement that married love in all its aspects is graceful, justifying, saving in itself, that God is there in the love of married persons for one another, brings affirmation to them of a sort not traditionally offered. That this grace experience is open to everyone, irrespective of faith or sacrament, is a most important insight, and I believe Rahner's powerful description of the partnership of love has freed the theologians following him to take up the questions of love and sexuality in the sacrament in the open way reflected in their writings.

Radically new in Mackin's theology is the willingness to address the role of sexual passion and pleasure in marriage in a positive light, and he is joined in this by Lawler. Their God is not lurking in the self sacrifice, in the putting up with the pain, the martyrdom to the institution that we have come to expect, but rather in the joy, in the unashamed passion, in the pleasure of the exchange of sexual love that can be at the heart of what is best in marriage between two people who love one another. The recognition that the expression of a man and woman in sexual love is not just a symbol, but can also be a making present of God's grace for the partners (and by implication for the wider community to which they belong – family first, and then society) must communicate a sense of being worthwhile in the eyes of God in terms that are meaningful to ordinary married people.

A criticism I would make of Mackin, Lawler and others is their unwillingness to treat in any depth the fact that, for some married people, the experience of sexuality can be devoid of the passion, pleasure and fulfillment they so joyfully describe. However, in pointing out the possibilities, it is reasonable to emphasise what is good, and the remaining impression is that with awareness, effort, and the grace/help of the sacrament, marriage can be a happy means to our hoped-for union with God for those who choose it.

The women theologians seem to be rooted in today's experience of marriage and the reality of the variety of households and relationships resulting from good and bad existential situations. Consequently the questioning of sexual intercourse within marriage as the norm for the expression of human sexuality is a logical progression and they rightly suggest that it should be faced honestly. Marriage in the scriptures and in the tradition is surely an important part of the Christian story, but we should keep in mind that we too are writing our chapter in the story as we live our marriages in this generation, or leave them and go on to new ways. We can do so sure in the knowledge that God will not abandon us in our search for truth, even if some of our routes refuse to be systematised in the eyes of those who would draw the maps for us all, and who insist that only the main roads be travelled.

Marriage in the church cannot be discussed in isolation from an overall view of faith in Christ, church, sacraments in general, moral theology, justice, and underlying all of it the nature of the human person as already graced in creation. This would ensure that, in marriage so grounded, any one-sided optimism concerning sexuality might be avoided, while celebrating in hope its goodness. With regard to the practical problem of indissolubility and the relationship of faith to sacrament, it seems to me that the starting place should perhaps be baptismal theology.

Theologians, Lehmann for example,[39] are aware of the inconsistency between sacramental theology and canon law in relation to faith and sacrament. Some choose to ignore it and assume that evangelisation prior to marriage will solve the problem. The logic of this may be that infant baptism should be discontinued, yet none of the theologians shows willingness to take the discussion back that far, in a way presuming that the non-believing baptised will, on being taught, come to sufficient faith to accept the inevitable sacramentality of their marriage. This seems unlikely, and so the search must continue in a spirit of acceptance of the tension between being open to a theology of marriage that is always in process, as people grow in understanding of what their married life means, and the human need to organise, to order marriage within the church and the world as institution that is identifiable, as sacrament that is truly a prayer of the church, and most importantly as relationship of persons that is an expression of God, Father, Christ and Spirit, with us.

Whether the evolving theology of marriage interacts well with contemporary Christian marriage will be considered in the final chapter.

Contemporary Christian Marriage and Theology of Marriage – A Helpful Interaction or Disconnected Worlds?

INTRODUCTION

In considering contemporary Christian marriage in the light of traditional theology, and more particularly of *recent* theology of marriage, the question at once arises as to whether the two are in touch with one another at all and, if they are, to what extent? In which areas of marriage is the theology meaningful, challenging, helpful to ordinary Christians living their marriages in today's world? Are there important facets of marriage today that are excluded from much of the theological reflection of even the most concerned and up-to-date theologians, whether married or not? Are the married Christians of today influenced by, or even open to, the notion of marriage that is taught by the church?

Christian marriage, as marriage in general, is perceived as being in crisis. The theology as surveyed in previous chapters continues to put forward the Christian view of marriage as a central factor in the Creator's design for humanity, and as a particular expression of Christian living whose aim is ultimately union with God through Christ. Fidelity, indissolubility and procreation are the hallmarks of Christian marriage today as they have always been, although with a perceptible change in emphasis. Is the ideal sufficiently grounded in the reality of ordinary marriages so as not to be completely out of touch? Are average

Christians in their marriage relationships sufficiently and realistically challenged and led on by the ideal? Can we relate to this ideal in any meaningful way? What aspects of traditional or modern theology of marriage are helpful and what hinder the bringing to reality of the aspirations of the average couple on their wedding day?

Undoubtedly some of the best features of modern theology are the attempts to understand sexuality and the affirmation of the goodness of sexual love as unitive as well as procreative in marriage. We also appreciate the encouraging of married Christians to speak from their explicitly married experience and to recognise that it can be a means to their finding God, which though different from the celibate way is not an inferior way. The cultural changes mentioned in chapter one, and particularly the feminist movement, contribute to the distance which may be perceived between theological language, with some of its concepts (for example the notion of headship in Ephesians), and the marriages of average Christians today.

Whether or not the language of theology is helpful, what can we draw on in terms of content from the traditional and recent theology? From the Old Testament accounts of creation we take the notion of the human pair as being made in God's image, that their delight in one another is part of the goodness of God's plan and leads to the capacity to create new life through their love. The *Song of Songs* and its celebration of erotic love easily finds a welcome in contemporary marriage where sexual fulfillment and love that is not necessarily procreative are priorities. The Wisdom literature and the writing of Hosea and other prophets stress that marriage is good, a blessing, and its meaning is not only that of the loving union of man and woman but is also a prophetic symbol, imaging the steadfast love of Yahweh for Israel. However, when the covenant image of Hosea is taken up by Paul in the New Testament and marriage of Christians takes on the gift(?) task(?) burden(?) of symbolising the unity of Christ and the church, with its indissolubility and its notion of husband as head of the wife, the connection between today's lived marriages and one of the central themes of marriage theology seems tenuous indeed. This I think is as much due to the entirely spiritual idea of the Christ/church unity as it is to the notion of husband as head of the wife. Perhaps if the incarnational reality of God with and in our world, which is central to Christian faith, was stressed to a greater degree, some of the difficulty in this regard might be overcome.

What of Augustine and his theology of marriage? Of all the Fathers of the church, Augustine, in our time of women's emancipation and sexual liberation, might be most easily dismissed as having nothing to say to us today. In spite of his erroneous beliefs about the female,[1] and his mistrust of human sexuality as a block to holiness, there is something in Augustine's writing that we need to hold fast to today perhaps more than ever. In an age of unprecedented sexual freedom such as ours, it is certainly unpopular to speak of sex and sin in the same breath. To suggest that, whatever about fornication and adultery, there may be sin in the sexual activity between married people would be to invite ridicule. Our church teaches that sexual expression and married sexual love is about giving, the 'mutual gifting of the partners' of *Gaudium et Spes*. If sexual exchange is without love, without the giving and receiving of the persons involved, then surely it misses its point? If this happens in marriage it does so to an even greater degree. Surely this missing of the basic point of sexuality as our means of reaching to another, and reaching to God in so doing, is precisely what sin is in the context of sex, whether within or outside of marriage? Is this not what Augustine meant by disordered use of sexuality, the result of concupiscence or selfish desire, being driven by our own passion rather than by shared passion? It is not passion itself that is sinful – it is surely among the greatest of God's gifts to humans. It is not sexual pleasure that is not good – lovers throughout the ages have known it to be precisely the opposite. The pursuit of these for self only, without due regard for the other, is what constitutes lust and not love, is what is flawed human behaviour, and this is as true today as it was in the time of Augustine.

A feature of the theology of marriage generally is that there is little understanding of the situation of women in marriage. In relatively recent years some women theologians have written with particular attention to the woman's view. It is surprising to find in Gregory of Nyssa's *De Virginitate* an insight and understanding of one aspect of marriage and motherhood of which any modern theologian might be proud.[2] Gregory's discussion on virginity and marriage is based on his distinction between possession and participation, attachment and non attachment. In speaking of the fear of loss/separation ever present in our enjoyment of everything in life, he writes of 'the mother who splits off her heart with the child, and if she becomes the mother of many, her soul is cut into as many parts as the number of her children, so as to feel in herself whatever happens to them'(3.5,10-6,17). From this it is easily seen how married women, especially mothers with their inability to detach, would long remain at the bottom of the scale with regard to virtue and capacity for holiness. Nonetheless, the value in understanding how things are with many mothers remains and can help in working towards a theology that is realistic for today's marriages.

From the medieval period, the most meaningful aspect is that marriage is a sacrament, that it is a means of grace for Christians. Also while today we might find some of the laws concerning marriage and the consent/consummation question very dispassionate, we can appreciate the need to organise which brought them about. This need is even more pressing today and this is one area where the law and theology need to find some way of relating to contemporary Christians as they serve the work of marriage tribunals, which are perceived, almost universally, as alienating for those who come into contact with them. This is not to suggest that disbanding the system is the answer, as some would want, but rather that a way of proceeding more in line with today's reality be pursued.[3]

The theology of marriage that can be called modern begins to address itself more directly to the personal aspects of marriage and so is more meaningful generally for the married today. However, although recent teaching shows progress in the notion of covenant as opposed to contract, and dares to use the word *love* in connection with marriage, I wonder whether the concept of marriage as image of Christ/church unity is not still removed from the world of many people. The ideal of marriage in the Christian view must, of course, be presented, but should it have to be filtered through several layers of interpretation by theologians to be made accessible to those it most concerns? The papers of the International Theological Commission, referred to in the previous chapter, show signs of some understanding of the reality of marriage today, and yet it is still my impression that the ordinary married are left to struggle with the meaning of what is probably the most challenging of the Christian states of life in our time. This is not to imply a competition between the difficulties of clerical or religious life and those of married life, but the faith needed to sustain marriage in the Christian sense, in today's cultural climate, is often not as strong as it needs to be, and many of the demands of Christian marriage only make sense in a context of strong faith.

PARTICULAR QUESTIONS

The Covenant image and the unity in marriage

The unity in Christian marriage that can image the unity of Christ and the church is certainly to be aimed at as an ideal, but in reality is it a possibility even for exceptionally dedicated Christian couples? The *Song of Songs* emphasises the celebration of the gift at the core of married love, the love that is beautiful, exciting, overwhelming, even before it is sustaining and creative, whose inward, outward and onward effects are a vehicle for God's presence and saving action in the world. But if the possibility for this celebration of humanity with God, which physical loving can be, is written into our being, there is also the possibility for the most degrading, dehumanising, person-destroying experiences, whose inward, outward and onward effects are only relatively recently being adverted to.[4] The extent of the personal and social problem that is domestic violence, and the ongoing effects of violent sexual assault, are only now being addressed openly, and perhaps only when this problem becomes political too will it begin to receive the attention needed to deal with it systematically. The reported declaration on the human rights of women from the 1995 UN Beijing Conference,[5] agreed by the Vatican representatives, may mark the beginning of a new realism in this regard as far as the church is concerned. Does Christian theology have anything to say to people who have been radically damaged by misuse of this gift of sexuality?

What of those whose experience of marriage is devoid of sexual passion, pleasure and fulfilment, who may not know anything of the joy that is so presumed in talk of married love? Is there a recognition that, within what may appear to be successful marriages, people may be living out lives of loneliness and great anguish, precisely because of the part this gift plays or does not play in their lives? Does theology understand that within average marriages there may be phases when this gift and its expression, or the frustration of it, may cause havoc in the best or worst sense, may cut right across the relationship of those involved?

What this seems to say is that what we do with this particular gift is central to the wellbeing and happiness of people. This is not to suggest that its full expression is essential for all, but it may be true to say that all of us are touched by it, perhaps far more than we realise. Dominian is the theologian most convinced of the pivotal place of sexual relationship in marriage, and his view would be shared by

Mackin and Lawler. Explicitly taking the opposite stance – that the sexual relationship should *not* be the be-all and end-all of marriage – are Thomas and Cahill.

Love and oneness

What then is the meaning of the oneness that is celebrated in the *Song of Songs*? The original oneness, which is the expression of harmony in Genesis and referred to by Jesus in the synoptic gospels, may be the experience of lovers in their private world, and yet it seems it must almost always be lost before it can be found again in the ongoing relationship that marriage is. Is the oneness of Christ and the church a meaningful, relevant, or even appropriate referent for it? Perhaps it is helpful in terms of fidelity in the Christian ideal of marriage, but I think that the absence of any physical or material connotation might well obscure its relevance for many married people. Love between men and women begins and is rooted in the physical. Oppenheimer reminds us that 'the physical is essentially the vehicle of the spiritual'.[6] Bernard Lonergan sees mutual love in marriage as the 'intertwining of two lives', the 'I' becomes a 'we', each attends, imagines, etc. in concern for both'.[7] Is this what love and marriage is? Is this so permanent? Is this truth or idealised love? If the early stage of such relationship is marked by oneness of a particular kind, a kind that says 'I can't tell where you end and I begin, where I end and you begin', and yet if the hope that it would last is not to be fulfilled, what is its meaning?

Is it that in this experience of oneness, men and women, with their fleeting glimpse of completion, of fulfillment and integration with another, of unity that is not a merging of persons and yet is so much more than co-operation, can have some apprehension of that permanent completion that can only be found in the one we understand to be God? In this closest possible union with another person we can be paradoxically most aware of the mystery that the other is, knowable and radically unknowable. The other is gift through whom we exist, through whom we take part in life itself, and through whom we are pointed beyond to the source of life itself, to God. Eric Fuchs writes:

> 'Because the other is and remains other even in a loving embrace, he(she) is both a harbor and a door: a place to anchor where everything – the whole world and our desire – takes on meaning, and an opening up into otherness, which is ultimately that of God.'[8]

William Butler Yeats, in a poem entitled 'Shadowy Waters', expresses the same idea more simply:

> Yet never have two lovers kissed but they
> Believed there was some other near at hand,
> And almost wept because they could not find it.[9]

Love and Conflict

If marriage in its ideal is primarily about the expression of love and the desire for unity of the couple (and recent theology well expresses this), in reality it is also about its frustration. It is about conflict, anger, justice and injustice, the struggle of two people to come to terms with their own being as individuals, and the attempt to make some sort of oneness out of their paired existence, which recent theology less well expresses.[10] If the sacrament of marriage is not just the wedding ceremony but the life of the couple, then it must include the whole life. Love and joy, peace and harmony are the obvious examples of the sacramental nature of marriage, but what of conflict and anger? Can they too be a means to holiness, a manifestation of the relationship between Christ and the church? Anger and the resulting conflict can lead people, perhaps especially married people, towards truth and integrity just as much as passionate lovemaking can. There is a nakedness and purity about anger that demands that we face the self and the other at the core, precisely *as this person*. We are challenged to listen, to hear the other, to hear the self, to know the self and the other in ways that may not be lovable. In conflict, in the unleashing of passion that anger can be, truth can emerge. A real meeting is possible through which the meaning of love must be re-examined, the reality of how the couple *are as couple* must be faced, and a decision about how they will be as a result of it must be taken. Here is where forgiveness and reconciliation, two fundamental characteristics of Christian relationship, may be experienced, given and received. The sacramentality of marriage is perhaps even more evident in the forgiving, accepting love that follows conflict than in a relationship that is always harmonious. Conflict can be an experience of grace, especially when we know love and acceptance along with the unpleasing truths about the self and the partner.

But conflict is not always an experience of grace and a means of growth. It may lead to truth and forgiveness, but it may also lead to a falsifying of the position between the couple, to a submerging of the truth of who the couple are and how they will be together as a result. The giving way to one another that Paul demands in Ephesians 5 may not always be the best way forward. To accomodate or to pacify the partner may not be what truth or honesty demands. E. and J. Whitehead understand conflict in marriage as leading the partners 'beyond individualism but not beyond integrity'.[11] Conflict can be the basis of change in the marriage relationship. It may be exciting in a good or negative sense. It may be constitutive of a downward spiral in the relationship. At worst, it can be habit-forming and is obviously entirely destructive if it becomes addictive or encompasses violence.

Love and justice

Christian theology of marriage continually presents the ideal of love to be striven for by those who would be followers of Jesus Christ. However this must be rooted in the real world of today's marriages if it is to be meaningful. Ideally, love needs no talk of rights or justice, and if marriages were in fact symbols of the covenant which unites God and humanity, Christ and the church, as much theology states, instead of being only *potential* symbols, a discussion on justice would be unnecessary. The reality is that neither of the partners in a marriage is God. Both are merely human, with all the faults and failings of the human condition, as well as the possibility of all that is best in humanity. Love must include justice. In a less than perfect marriage, or phase of a marriage, justice and the demand for it by either or both partners has its place. The human person is an individual first and foremost, and the greatest degree of intimacy in marriage does not change the fact that each person must be accorded the same dignity and rights as all others. In our contemporary world, women have begun to claim their rights as human persons both in marriage and outside of it. Changes in our way of living, the raising of consciousness, the availability of contraception, opportunities of different sorts, are emerging and yet are still out of reach of many women. All give new meaning to the love that must include justice in the marriage relationship. This justice is not to be confused with charity, nor with indulgence, but must give to each partner his or her due, given all the factors influencing the relationship of each couple. It particularly does not mean rights in the traditionally used sense of marriage theology – rights over one another's bodies, perpetual, exclusive or any other kind. This notion as a model for marriage appalls in today's atmosphere of marriage based on mutual love. Love, most especially sexual love, is freely given and received or it must be called by some other name. In marriage, love and justice need to be spoken of together and in our day with particular emphasis on justice for women in marriage. The balance, however, needs to be maintained. If you talk only of love, the likelihood is that you end in sentimentality. If you talk of justice only you may end with self-righteousness.[12]

It is undoubtedly true that in today's marriage the claiming of justice by women particularly is having a profound effect on the lives of many families. Expectations are high. Many women are no longer willing to accept a role that was considered appropriate in previous generations – that of full-time service of the physical, emotional, psychological and even spiritual needs of husbands and children, to the practical obliteration of their own. The institution of marriage, Christian and otherwise, is adapting slowly to the justice demands of women to be equal partners. At present, lip service is paid to their rights both by church and society. The reality, as testified to by women writers, is that progress is slow and painful, and for many women simply not worth the ongoing struggle.[13]

There are hopeful signs emerging however. The 1994 lenten pastoral letter of Desmond Connell, Archbishop of Dublin, entitled *Catholic Family Life*, explicitly refers to the frequent exploitation of mothers by their husbands and children with regard to the responsibility for the ordinary running of the home and of family life, and calls for more equal participation in all that is involved.[14] And another welcome contribution to this question of women and justice is *Women in the Church: An Issue of Solidarity*, written by a group of Jesuits based in Dublin. This theological reflection on the situation of women in the church and in society addresses the questions of co-responsibility of men with women in issues affecting family life and the matter of violence against women, among others.[15]

Love and creativity

In Christian theology the link between love in marriage and the procreation of new life is strongly maintained. If marriage is no longer seen as primarily for the purpose of generating new life, the reality is that for most couples the conception, birth and rearing of children is perhaps the most obvious expression of the inward, outward and onward thrust of their love. The 'throughness' of children in a marriage (well understood by Gregory of Nyssa) is the permanent reminder of the creativity of love. And yet children are not the goal of this love, but rather its gift. For many couples today, and for many reasons, love's creativity will find expression in ways other than the conception and birth of children. Love is for sharing, and whether or not a family has children, the creative nature of love means that its effects will reach beyond the boundaries of family in the narrow sense and will involve the wider community in a variety of ways.[16]

It seems right to mention here that there is a negative possibility for marriage today in that privatisation, rather than personalisation, may result sometimes from its de-institutionalisation. The move to a more personal approach can sometimes be the cause of almost the entire energy of the couple being focused inwards on themselves and their own needs to the exclusion of anything or anyone else. It would seem that this might be more of a problem where children are not part of the marriage intention, but the possibility is also there for those who have children, and some aspects of modern life and work patterns may be constitutive of the problem.

Love, commitment and exclusivity

The creativity of love may express itself in other inter-personal relationships or activities of the partners outside the marriage. E. and J. Whitehead point out that commitment in marriage is not to emotional exclusivity, but does involve priority and permanence. They stress that 'priority and permanence are not automatic guarantees of marriage but the fruit of a lively relationship.'[17] In this regard, I think some more open discussion about what marriage is about, what precisely exclusivity means, what we are to be with and for one another and the wider world, would be helpful. No one relationship – that of being wife or husband, mother or father, colleague or friend – can encompass the whole of a person, and yet at the moment we try to give our all to each. In today's climate of change and confusion over roles in marriage it is important to look honestly at the commitment that marriage is. Does the committed sexual relationship forge a particular bond, not just in law but in fact – despite the reality that it may not work out in the long run?[18] What do we owe our children? Is the traditional idea of exclusivity in marriage oppressive and even a contributory factor to marriage breakdown as husband or wife looks for all needs to be satisfied in one relationship? Would it be more helpful to recognise the desirability of other relationships outside of marriage first, and then to work out what form these might appropriately take? Would it be more helpful to examine the reality of relationships and see which include giving and receiving and which are more about taking; which are genuinely out of love's overflow and which are out of whatever need of our own? That is not to say that need is wrong of itself, that married people should not involve in relationships out of need that is not met in the marriage, but an honesty in facing the truth of other relationships might be appropriate and helpful in the long run. Friendship, particularly deep friendship with someone of the other sex, can be difficult to deal with in some marriages or in some phases of a marriage. Ben Kimmerling points out the implications with regard to the primary commitment to the partner and sees genuine unselfish giving as the possible outcome of such relationship.[19]

There remains much to be learned about friendship and how we are as human persons, how to handle intimate friendship and our sexuality in the context of a close relationship other than that with husband or wife. Do we approach friendship with fear of what may and often does happen – emotional involvement that leads to conflicting feelings of guilt and rightness – if our basic commitment is to another? Or can we approach others with love, accepting that things may go astray sometimes, and that sometimes through the apparently astray truth may be reached? The frustration of the natural outreaching of people who love and are loved can have far-reaching negative effects in marriage. Some people retreat into the protective shell of the marriage and limit all to there. Some involve themselves in driven activity which can wear the mask of charitable action. Others still cope by over emotional involvement in their children, which can be destructive and lead to their incapacity to form relationships of their own.

Dominian, in his recent book on marriage, presents a compassionate account of trust and its betrayal in marriage, of infidelity and its causes and possible outcome.[20] While he emphasises that forgiveness is centrally important for all

Christians, and gives an understanding account of the problem which infidelity in marriage is today, I wonder whether in pointing out so well the good that may be for the individual in adultery, he does not contribute to the further weakening of the institution of marriage for society at large. This is not to suggest that adultery is the worst offence a spouse can commit against her/his partner, but if Christians are to take the ideal of marriage and family seriously perhaps more emphasis on commitment, and even conflict where necessary in confronting problems, might encourage today's couples to invest more effort in their own marriage relationship, with consequent benefit to themselves, their family and the wider world.

CONCLUSION

The theology of marriage has much to offer to today's couples as they seek to live out their commitment to the Christian ideal. Nevertheless, the incalculable difficulty of living two lives as one should never be underestimated by those who set the guidelines. Where is the oneness at its best? I return to the *Song of Songs* and its claim. The possibility is there, in the God-given oneness that is at the heart of marriage as intended, for our reaching to our goal which is union with God. There also is the basis to give freely to the other not only oneself but the self of the other, to discover in an ongoing way who each is.

The love of the *Song of Songs*, of youth and beauty, is a love that is stronger than death, but it is not suggestive of a repression or inability to love others. If this bond of early relationship is lived to the full, seen in its full potential as the gift it is, then it may be experienced as stronger than death and other relationships which are also good gift will be enjoyed.

Do we set ourselves impossible ideals as Christians and as human in the world? What if love fails, if the love of humans proves to be less enduring than the love of God it is said to signify? Love is the basis of most marriages,

Christian or otherwise. If the very basis of the bond between the couple ceases to exist, can they be said to image Christ and the church as united? Should we accept the human in ourselves and not pretend that the ideal is there for all who only have to want it? This is not to suggest that we should not strive for the ideal but it seems that, for too many people, the institution is more important than the individual persons involved in it. Enforced martyrdom to the institution of marriage may lead to a less than accurate view of God's forgiving love. Could it be that the absolute upholding of the institution in every instance is responsible, not for safeguarding the truth but perhaps for the spread of a flawed Christianity? Could it be that we have something to learn from the way the question of divorce and remarriage is handled in the Orthodox church, referred to in the previous chapter?

The theology of marriage says to the married of today, as it has said since the beginning, that their relationship has the capacity to symbolise the faithful, forgiving and enduring love of God. It is my impression that the married Christians of today will find meaning in much of the theology, while at the same time recognising that both marriage itself and theology are evolving towards new ways of expressing the essential oneness of God with humanity.

Some concluding observations

In the final chapter a section entitled *Love and Youth* might have been pertinent, because it seems to me that a problem with the theology of marriage and its reception is that it is mainly written by the middle-aged, if not in some cases by elderly Christians. (Whether these are married or celibate may be of secondary importance here.) How are we to allow for people to make mistakes? The radical incapacity to conceive of some aspects of how this or that marriage might turn out, and so to know what marriage is, should give pause as far as proposing absolutes is concerned. Is it at all meaningful to discuss it in traditional terms – at least for today's younger people? Is Christian marriage simply a wanting to be with, a confirming of something, and despite differing degrees of faith – little, less, or much – the wish to manifest it in this context?

The question of admitting the divorced and remarried to Communion becomes more pressing. How often did Jesus cause scandal? If the possibility of giving scandal to those already favoured becomes the measure of concern and care for the wounded in our church, what kind of church have we got? It seems to me that there is urgent need for a more positive and welcoming approach towards people in objectively irregular situations. The pastoral care that Pope John Paul called for in *Familiaris Consortio* is notable too often by its absence.[21]

Questions remain to be pursued in the area of sexuality. For example, Lawler moves the debate on. Perhaps he is right in saying that it is not realistic to idealise sex and its expression in marriage, but one might pose the question as to whether this is true to the same extent for women. This in turn raises the question of the differing sexual responses of women and whether Lawler might be inclined to making the male sexual response normative.

A liberation theology of marriage, a retrieval of utopia, as in Gutierrez, applied to marriage (not limited to the sexual) might be one way to look to the future.[22] This concept of utopia is not referring to some impossible dream, but is precisely rooted in present reality and is open to imaginative and rational possibility. If, based on Genesis, the new covenant marriage that is Christian marriage is to unite what has been torn asunder, to find the way to harmony and peace, then for Christians the belief that it is possible to come close to it in daily living is crucial. This may mean the willingness and capacity to endure the necessary battles within the individual as individual (the 'that which I will I do not' of St Paul) and also within the couple as pair – (*we* do not do what *we* want, what *we* will not *we* do). Is it an impossible task? Left alone it would seem so, but as members of the group of Christians, the church, with what is implied by the presence of Christ/Spirit, maybe it is not altogether impossible. To be habitually honest, just, loving and so on is an extremely difficult project in any lifetime but, perhaps, if these moments are grasped and really lived, the basis for such living can be present more often than not. To be fully present in the best moments of marriage, just as much as in the difficulties, to name them, live them, praise God in them, might go a long way towards the realisation of the goals of Christian marriage.

If these goals are truly from and oriented to God, then fear of difference, or change in the working out of how they are to be achieved, is not necessary. New ways and new meanings in different cultural contexts could be welcomed instead of being seen as a source of threat to stability, which can sometimes mask stagnation. The words of John F. Haught (in *What is God?*) about beauty and our way of being in the world seem to me to be especially helpful and appropriate for those contemplating marriage, or already married and experiencing the tension between freedom and constraint, individuality and community, that it brings:

> Do not settle for an order that is too narrow for you. By all means follow your passion for order since without order there is nothingness. But strive for an order that is tolerant of novelty and conflicts.
>
> The ultimately satisfying order is not a harmony attained by suppressing conflict among the elements that make it up.
>
> Be open to novelty even if it produces a temporary discord, for in the larger scheme of things that lies beyond your comprehension, beauty will prevail.
>
> Ultimate beauty will insure that all manner of things shall be well.[23]

Notes

INTRODUCTION

1 A. Greeley, 'Empirical Liturgy – The Search for Grace', *America*, Nov. 1987.

CHAPTER I

1 W. Kasper, *Theology of Christian Marriage*, tr, London: Burns and Oates, 1980, 5.

2 Ibid., 6.

3 Augustine, *De Bono Coniugali*, xxiv. *The Works of St Augustine, Anti Pelagian Writings* Vol 2. Ed. Rev. Marcus Dodds, D.D., Edinburgh: 1874.

4 E. and J. Whitehead, *Marrying Well*, New York: Image Books, 1983, 20-21.

5 E. Schillebeeckx, *Marriage: Human Reality and Saving Mystery*, London: Sheed and Ward, 1965, xvi, xvii.

6 Ibid., xvii.

7 W. Kasper, op. cit., 9.

8 E. Schillebeeckx, *Marriage: Human Reality and Saving Mystery*. See the general Introduction XVII for development of this point. Kasper, ch.1, 9-12, and E. and J. Whitehead, ch. 3, 'Marriage in Transition', 43-44, also make this point.

9 J. Dominian, *Passionate and Compassionate Love*, London: Darton, Longman and Todd, 1991, 26-27.

10 See for example *Parent's Booklet*, Eastern Health Board, Child Abuse Prevention Programme (1991).

11 J. Dominian, op. cit., 27.

12 F. Robertson Elliot, *The Family: Change or Continuity?* London: Macmillan Education, 1986. Discussion with table in ch. 6, 'Remodelling the Conjugal Family'.

13 Elliot deals with this at some length in ch. 4, 'Marriage, Parenthood and Gender Divisions'.

14 M. Lawler, *Secular Marriage Christian Sacrament*, Connecticut: Twenty Third Publications, 1985, 18.

15 Lawler, op. cit, 69.

16 K. Rahner, *Theological Investigations*, Vol 10, tr, New York: Herder and Herder, 1973, 199-221 at 201.

17 H. Oppenheimer, *Marriage*, London: Mowbray, 1990, 62. This will be dealt with in more detail in a subsequent section.

18 Rahner, op. cit, 205.

CHAPTER II

1 E. Schillebeeckx, *Marriage: Human Reality and Saving Mystery*, London: Sheed and Ward, 1965, 13.

2 K. Barth, *Church Dogmatics*, Vol 111, Part 4, 'The Doctrine of Creation', tr, Edinburgh: T. & T. Clark, 1961, 140.

3 J. Dominian, *Marriage, Faith and Love*, London: Darton, Longman and Todd Ltd., 1984, 10. W. Kasper, *Theology of Christian Marriage*, tr, London: Burns and Oates Ltd., 1980, 26.

4 J. Dominian, op. cit., 11.

5 Ibid., 11.

6 R.E. Murphy, in *The New Jerome Biblical Commentary*, London: Chapman, 1989, 462-3. M. Pope, *Song of Songs*, Anchor Bible, New York: Doubleday, 1977, 18,19.

7 E. Schillebeeckx, op.cit., 55.

8 Ibid., 59-60.

9 Tobit 8:5-9, I. Nowell, *New Jerome Biblical Commentary*, London: Chapman, 1989, 571. Nowell writes that it should be presumed that the marriage is consummated on the wedding night.The tradition of the three nights of continence is derived from the Vulgate but not found in the Greek recensions.

10 M. Lawler, op. cit., 8.

11 E. Schillebeeckx, op. cit., 40-42.

12 M. Lawler, op. cit., 10.

13 Ibid., 11.

14 See Lawler, p 86. The dispute between the schools of Hillel and Shammai concerned the interpretation of the expression 'erwat dabar' – something indecent for which a husband had the

right to dismiss his wife. The Shammai ruling was to interpret it strictly. Only moral or sexual delinquency justified divorce. The Hillel school, by contrast, took a very broad view, allowing divorce for what might be trivial reasons.

15 D. Rops, *Daily Life in Palestine at the Time of Christ*, tr, London: Weidenfeld and Nicolson, 1962, 116-7.

16 A recent and very full treatment of this issue is Raymond Collins' *Divorce in the New Testament*, Minnesota: Liturgical Press, 1992.

17 E. Schüssler Fiorenza, *In Memory of Her*, New York: Crossroad, 1984, 15.

18 M. Barth, *Ephesians 4-6*, Anchor Bible, New York: Doubleday, 1974, 676, 703.

19 E. Fuchs, *Sexual Desire and Love*, tr, New York: Seabury Press, 1983, 75.

20 J. Dominian, *Passionate and Compassionate Love*, London: Darton, Longman and Todd, 1991, 22.

21 K. Barth, *Church Dogmatics*, Vol 111, Part 4, tr, Edinburgh: T. & T. Clark, 1961, 148.

22 *Song Of Songs*, 7:6-9.

23 *Song of Songs*, 7:10-13.

24 R. Hanson, *Allegory and Event*, London: SCM, 1959, 115-117.

25 M. Pope, *Song of Songs*, Anchor Bible, New York: Doubleday, 1977, 115.

26 Ibid., 116-120.

27 Ibid., 120.

28 In fairness to the great mystics one must recognise their need to try to give expression to their experience. What other language could have conveyed their joy and delight at their experience of God? In the end maybe there is no other way to speak of it, but the effect of the 'theft' is in some way to make less of love between man and woman whose language it properly is. Barth writes dismissively of Schleiermacher for his 'theologising of eros' and his 'eroticising of theology', but it seems to me that the distinctions are not so easily delineated. For Schleiermacher 'it must be God who is manifested in lovers. Their embrace is really His embrace …' (*Lucindenbriefe*, 495), quoted by Barth in *Church Dogmatics* Vol 111, 122. Barth sees this as exalting man to the deity, leaving him without a master, abandoned by God.

29 M. Lawler, op. cit., 29.

30 T. Mackin, *The Marital Sacrament*, New York: Paulist Press, 1989, 206-210.

31 T. Mackin, op. cit., 201-206.

32 Augustine, *On the good of Marriage*, Fathers of the Church 27, R. Deferrari, ed., tr, Washington: Catholic University of America Press, 1955, 47, 48.

33 Augustine, *De Nuptiis et Concupiscentia*, in *The Works of St Augustine: Anti Pelagian Writings* Vol 2, ed: Rev. Marcus Dodds D.D., Edinburgh: 1874.

34 Augustine, *De Continentia*, F C 16:169.

35 Augustine, *De Bono Conjugali*, ch. 23.

36 P. Elliott, *What God Has Joined:The Sacramentality of Marriage*, New York: Alba House, 1990, 160. Elliott would like to rediscover the 'meaning of the unchanged teaching of the magisterium on the higher value of virginity.'

37 D. M. Thomas, *Christian Marriage*, New York: Image Books, 1983, 88.

38 M. Lawler, op. cit., 36-37.

39 R. Brooke, *The Medieval Idea of Marriage*, Oxford: University Press, 1991, ch. 2, 'The Inheritance, Christian and Roman'.

40 Brooke, op. cit., 120-125.

41 D. Thomas, op. cit., 90.

42 Lawler, op. cit., 37-40. Thomas, op. cit., 90.

43 J. Noonan, *Powers to Dissolve*, Mass: Harvard University Press, 1972, Preface xv.

44 Mackin, in *The Marital Sacrament*, (ch. 10, footnote 70, 447), points out that Trent sought to anathematise Luther, while avoiding doing the same to the Orthodox Church which allowed divorce because of adultery, and remarriage.

45 T. O'Loughlin, 'Adam's Rib and the Equality of the Sexes: Some Medieval Exegesis of Gen 2:21-22'. Unpublished article March 1992.

CHAPTER III

1 Canons 1055, 1056 of *The Code of Canon Law*, tr, London: Collins Liturgical Publications, 1983.

2 M. Lawler, *Secular Marriage, Christian Sacrament*, Connecticut: Twenty Third Publications, 1985, 44.

3 Ibid., 46, 47.

4 D. Thomas, *Christian Marriage*, Delaware: Glazier, 1983, 113.

5 Lawler, op. cit., 47, 48. Reference to Von Hildebrand, *Marriage*, London: Longmans, Green and Co., 1942, v, vi.

6 Lawler, ibid. Reference to Doms, *The Meaning of Marriage*, tr, London: Sheed and Ward 1939, 94-95.

7 T. Mackin, *What is Marriage?* New York: Paulist Press, 1982, 231-235.

8 *Gaudium et Spes*. The first chapter of Part Two of the document is entitled 'The Dignity of Marriage and the Family'. Par 48 develops the theme of marriage as covenant.

9 The 1917 Code also describes marriage in terms of consent, but the context is that of contract.

10 T. Mackin, *The Marital Sacrament*, New York: Paulist Press, 1989, 621.

11 Ibid., 589.

12 Ibid., 594. Mackin here refers to Scheeben, *The Theology of the Mystical Body*, St Louis, 1957, (tr) 601-602.

13 Ibid., 602-614 and 622. Mackin gives a detailed presentation of Schillebeeckx's theology of marriage as it develops in his writing. This last thesis from the 1974 essay is on p. 622.

14 K. Rahner, 'Marriage as Sacrament', *Theological Investigations*, Vol 10, tr, original 1967, New York: Herder and Herder, 1973, 199-221.

15 Ibid., 203.

16 T. Mackin, 'How to Understand the Sacrament of Marriage', in *Commitment to Partnership*, W. Roberts, ed., New Jersey: Paulist Press, 1987, 34-60. Also, *The Marital Sacrament*, New York: Paulist Press, 1989. J. Dominian, 'Christian Marriage' in *Commitment to Partnership,* 158-166. M. Lawler, op. cit., ch. 4, 72-77.

17 This is a constant theme in the writing of Dominian on marriage in general and on Christian marriage in particular. His recent work, *Passionate and Compassionate Love*, London: Darton, Longman and Todd, 1991, treats marriage and the family as a community of love in which God is to be found.

18 J. Dominian, op. cit., 94.

19 Ibid., 95.

20 M. Lawler, op. cit.

21 M. Lawler, op. cit., 72.

22 A question I share with Lawler.

23 Rosemary Haughton in *The Passionate God*, New York: Paulist Press, 1981, cited in Thomas, *Christian Marriage*, Delaware: Glazier, 1983, also relates our human passion to God's passionate love for us.

24 T. Mackin, op. cit., 52.

25 Malone and Connery, eds., *Contemporary Perspectives on Christian Marriage*, Chicago: Loyola University Press, 1984, Original 1978.

26 Ibid., 84.

27 Lehmann, 'The Sacramentality of Christian Marriage', in Malone and Connery, op. cit.

28 Ibid., 100-111.

29 C. Caffarra, 'Marriage as a Reality in the Order of Creation and Marriage as Sacrament', in Malone and Connery, op. cit., 177-179.

30 P. Delhaye, 'Nature and Grace in the Theology of Vatican II: A Note on Caffarra's Marriage as a Reality in the Order of Creation and Marriage as Sacrament', in Malone and Connery, op. cit., 285-295.

31 W. Roberts, ed., *Commitment to Partnership*, New Jersey: Paulist Press, 1987, 81-99.

32 Cahill, op. cit., 89.

33 Ibid., 90.

34 Ibid., 95.

35 R. Haughton, 'Marriage in Women's New Consciousness', in Roberts, op. cit., 141-157 at 149.

36 K. Kelly, *Divorce and Second Marriage: Facing the Challenge*, London: Collins, 1982.

37 For further reading on the position of the Orthodox Church see John Meyendorff, *Marriage: An Orthodox Perspective*, New York: St Vladimir's Seminary Press, 1975, 60-65. Also, for a more recent discussion, see Theodore Stylianopolous, 'The Indissolubility of Marriage in The New Testament: Principles and Practise', *Greek Orthodox Theological Review*, Vol 34, no 4, 1989, 335-345.

38 P. Elliott, *What God Has Joined: The Sacramentality of Marriage*, New York: Alba House, 1990, 212.

39 Lehmann, 'The Sacramentality of Christian Marriage', in Malone and Connery, op. cit.

CHAPTER IV

1 See Anna M. Wilson, 'Augustine on the Status of Women', in *Milltown Studies*, No 19 & 20, Spring/Autumn 1987, 87-109.

2 Mark D. Hart, 'Gregory of Nyssa's Theology of Marriage' in *Theological Studies* 1990, 452-477. However, in pointing out why virginity is advantageous, Gregory shows a poor opinion of those who marry. Marriage is 'the common starting point of error' concerning what is truly valuable.

3 See M. McGuckian, SJ, 'Dual Marriages – An Alternative to Divorce?' *Studies*, Winter 1991, 388-399. Although writing about Civil Law the points he makes concern Christian marriage.

4 In the Irish context, Ben Kimmerling addresses this question in an article entitled 'Amongst Women', *The Furrow*, Vol 44, No 5, May 1993.

5 As reported in the *Irish Times*, September 11th 1995.

6 H. Oppenheimer, *Marriage*, London: Mowbray, 1990, 63.

7 B. Lonergan, *Method in Theology*, London: Darton, Longman and Todd, 1972, 433.

8 E. Fuchs, *Sexual Desire and Love*, tr, original 1979, New York: Seabury Press, 1983, 203. A fuller treatment is in the section 'The Spiritual Value of Eroticism', 192-209.

9 W. B. Yeats, 'The Shadowy Waters', A Dramatic Poem, *The Collected Poems of W.B. Yeats*, London: Macmillan, 1933, 479.

10 I have borrowed the term 'paired existence' from Sinead Twomey in an unpublished essay, 'Marriage: A Paired Existence' written for an undergraduate philosophy course assignment.

11 E. and J. Whitehead, *Marrying Well*, Garden City: Doubleday, 1981, 226. The section on intimacy shows times of conflict and disagreement to be valuable as much as idyllic moments. This kind of intimacy leads to the possibility of change in the individual, invites beyond the self.

12 David Tracy's way of speaking of love and justice (at a seminar on the Trinity, in Trinity College Dublin, March 1992) seems very pertinent in relation to marriage.

13 See Cahill on *Familiaris Consortio*, in *Commitment To Partnership*, and F. Robertson Elliot in *Family: Change or Continuity?* as examples, in references already cited.

14 The Most Reverend Desmond Connell, DD, Archbishop of Dublin, *Catholic Family Life*, Pastoral Letter, Lent 1994, 9-10.

15 Brian Lennon SJ, Gerry O'Hanlon SJ, Bill Toner SJ, Frank Sammon SJ, *Women In The Church: An Issue of Solidarity*, Dublin: Jesuit Centre for Faith and Justice, 1995, 11,12.

16 E. and J. Whitehead, (op. cit., 89,90,91), referring to Augustine's goods of marriage, treat fruitfulness as internal (mutual love, fidelity), external (children) and transcendent (sacrament, lasting love makes visible the enduring, faithful presence of God).

17 Ibid., 331.

18 M. McGuckian, in the paper already cited, argues for indissolubility at the expense of exclusivity, and that second marriage is preferable to divorce.

19 B. Kimmerling, 'Sexual Love and the Love of God: A Spirituality of Sexuality,' in *Doctrine and Life*, 35, 1986, 454-465.

20 J. Dominian, op. cit., 145-150.

21 John Hosie SM, in *Catholics, Divorce and Remarriage*, Sydney: E. J. Dwyer, 1993, gives a lead in this regard. His clear and compassionate treatment of the issues includes in full the 1982 statement of the New Zealand bishops, *When Dreams Die*. This document could be studied and reflected on at diocesan and parish level with much benefit to everyone affected by marriage breakdown, whether existentially or pastorally.

22 G. Gutierrez, *A Theology of Liberation: History, Politics and Salvation*, tr, Maryknoll: Orbis, 1973, 236.

23 J. Haught, *What is God?*, Dublin: Gill and Macmillan, 1985, 91.

Bibliography

Augustine, *De Nuptiis et Concupiscentia*, in *The Works of St Augustine*, Anti Pelagian Writings Vol 2, Ed. M. Dodds, Edinburgh, 1874.

On The Good of Marriage, Fathers of The Church, 27. A New Translation. R. Deferrari ed., Washington: Catholic University of America Press, 1955.

De Continentia, Fathers of The Church, 16. A New Translation. R. Deferrari ed., Washington: Catholic University of America Press, 1952.

Barth, K., *Church Dogmatics* Vol III, The Doctrine of Creation, Edinburgh: T. & T. Clark, 1961.

Barth, M., *Ephesians 4-6*, Anchor Bible, New York: Doubleday, 1974.

Brooke, R., *The Medieval Idea of Marriage*, Oxford University Press, 1991.

Collins, R., *Divorce in the New Testament*, Minnesota: Liturgical Press, 1992.

Dominian, J., *Marriage, Faith and Love*, London: Darton, Longman and Todd, 1984.

Dominian, J., *Passionate and Compassionate Love*, London: Darton, Longman and Todd, 1991.

Elliot, F. Robertson, *The Family: Change or Continuity?* London: Macmillan Education, 1986.

Elliott, P., *What God Has Joined: The Sacramentality of Marriage*, New York: Alba House, 1990.

Fiorenza, E. Schüssler, *In Memory of Her*, New York: Crossroad, 1984.

Fuchs, E., *Sexual Desire and Love*, tr, New York: Seabury Press, 1983.

Gutierrez, G., *A Theology of Liberation: History, Politics and Salvation*, tr, Maryknoll: Orbis, 1973.

Hanson, R., *Allegory and Event*, London: SCM Press Ltd., 1959.

Hosie, J., *Catholics, Divorce and Remarriage*, Sydney: E. J. Dwyer, 1991.

Kasper, W., *Theology of Christian Marriage*, tr, London: Burns and Oates, 1980.

Kelly, K., *Divorce and Second Marriage*, London: Collins, 1982.

Lawler, M., *Secular Marriage, Christian Sacrament*, Connecticut: Twenty Third Publications, 1985.

Lonergan, B., *Method in Theology*, London: Darton, Longman and Todd, 1982.

Mackin, T., *What is Marriage?* New York: Paulist Press, 1982.

Mackin, T., *The Marital Sacrament*, New York: Paulist Press, 1989.

Malone, R., and Connery, J. eds, *Contemporary Perspectives on Christian Marriage*, Chicago: Loyola University Press, 1984.

Meyendorff, J., *Marriage: An Orthodox Perspective*, New York: St Vladimir's Seminary Press, 1975.

Noonan, J., *Powers To Dissolve*, Mass.: Harvard University Press, 1972.

Oppenheimer, H., *Marriage*, London: Mowbray, 1990.

Pope, M., *Song of Songs*, Anchor Bible, New York: Doubleday, 1977.

Rahner, K., *Theological Investigations*, Vol 10, tr, New York: Herder and Herder, 1973.

Roberts, W., ed., *Commitment to Partnership*, New Jersey: Paulist Press, 1987.

Rops, D., *Daily Life in Palestine at the Time of Christ*, tr, Weidenfield and Nicholson, 1962.

Schillebeeckx, E., *Marriage: Human Reality and Saving Mystery*, London: Sheed and Ward, 1965.

Thomas, D., *Christian Marriage*, New York: Image Books, 1983.

Whitehead, E. and J., *Marrying Well*, New York: Image Books, 1983.

Yeats, W. B., *The Collected Poems of W. B.Yeats*, London: Macmillan, 1933.

Articles

Greeley, A., 'Empirical Liturgy – The Search for Grace', *America*, Nov. 1987.

Hart, M.D., 'Gregory of Nyssa's Theology of Marriage',\ *Theological Studies*, 1990.

Kimmerling, B., 'Sexual Love and the Love of God: A Spirituality of Sexuality', *Doctrine and Life*, 35, 1986.

Kimmerling, B., 'Amongst Women', *The Furrow*, Vol 44, No 5, May 1993.

McGuckian, M., 'Dual Marriages – An Alternative to Divorce?', *Studies*, Winter 1991.

McGuckian, M., 'A Case Against Incapacity Annulments.' Unpublished article, Feb. 1992.

Murphy, R., 'Canticle of Canticles', *New Jerome Biblical Commentary*, London: Chapman, 1989.

Nowell, I., 'Tobit, Judith, Ester', *New Jerome Biblical Commentary*, London: Chapman, 1989.

O' Loughlin, T., 'Adam's Rib and the Equality of the Sexes: Some Medieval Exegesis of Gen 2:21–22'. Unpublished article, March, 1992.

Stylianopolous, T., 'The Indissolubility of Marriage in the New Testament: Principles and Practise', *Greek Orthodox Theological Review*, Vol 34, No 4, 1989.

Twomey, S., 'Marriage: A Paired Existence'. Unpublished essay, 1986.

Pamphlets
Parent's Booklet, Eastern Health Board, Child Abuse Prevention Programme, 1991.

Familiaris Consortio, Apostolic Exhortation of Pope John Paul II, tr, London: C. T. S., 1981.

Letter issued in advance of UN World Conference on Women 1995, July.

Gaudium et Spes, tr, *Vatican Council II, The Conciliar and Post Conciliar Documents*, A. Flannery, ed., Dublin: Dominican Publications, 1975.

Catholic Family Life, Pastoral Letter of Desmond Connell, Archbishop of Dublin, Lent 1994.

Women in the Church, Lennon, O'Hanlon, Toner & Sammon, Dublin: Jesuit Centre for Faith and Justice, 1995.